BILL PORTLOCK

Hello, Hampton Roads

BY GUY FRIDDELL

Designed by

ALAN JACOBSON

Editorial Consultants

LOUIS D. RUBIN JR.   RUTH WALKER

Printed by

W.M. BROWN AND SON, INC., RICHMOND, VIRGINIA

Distributed by

DIETZ PRESS, RICHMOND, VIRGINIA

Published by

THE FUTURE OF HAMPTON ROADS, INC.

Represented by

DALE BOWEN   THOMAS P. CHISMAN   HENRY CLAY HOFHEIMER   WILLIAM WILKINSON

To the photographers

WILLIAM ABOURJILIE
MARK ATKINSON
TOM BENNETT
CATHY DIXSON
RAYMOND GEHMAN
BILL KELLEY II
MIKE LANE

PAUL AIKEN
HERB BARNES
LOIS BERNSTEIN
RICHARD DUNSTON
ROBERT HART
MICHAEL KESTNER
JOHN LOIZIDES
MICHELE MCDONALD

RICHARD ANDERSON
M.L. BARNETT
BOB BROWN
MORT FRYMAN
DAVID HOLLINGSWORTH
SCOTT KINGSLEY
GLEN MCCLURE

Whose lenses lent loveliness herein

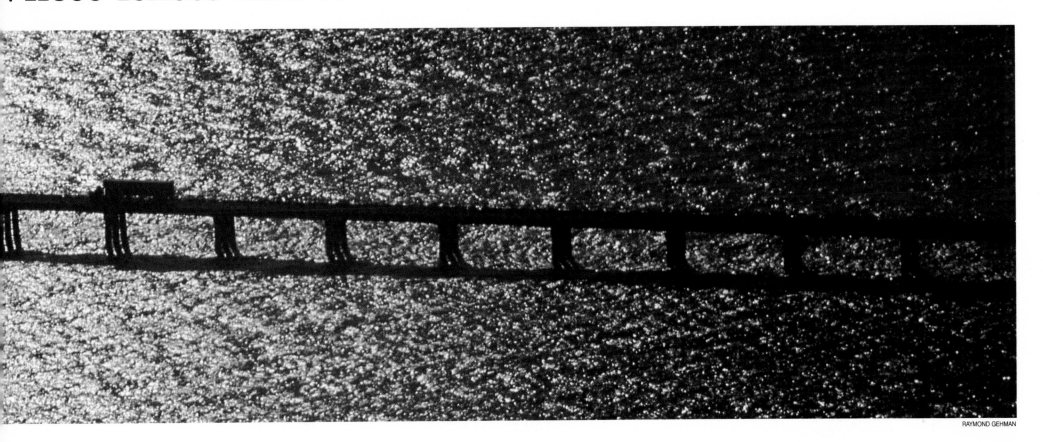

RAYMOND GEHMAN

KEVIN MCPARTLAND

CRAIG L. MORAN

L. FLOYD NOCK

BILL PORTLOCK

MARTIN RODDEN

JOHN H. SHEALLY II

ERIC THINGSTAD

MARK MITCHELL

LYTTON J. MUSSELMAN

CHRIS OXLEY

TOMMY PRICE

LINDY KEAST RODMAN

KENNETH STUTZ

BILL TIERNAN

MIKE WILLIAMS

DENNIS MOOK

ANN MYERS

JIM PILE

ROBIE RAY

PAUL SCHNABEL

DENNIS TENNANT

KAREN D. TWIDDY

Above, a lone truck crossing the 17.6-mile Chesapeake Bay Bridge-Tunnel accents the immensity of the Bay and the sparkling ocean beyond.

3

Contents

Cover photos: Bay-Bridge Tunnel and beach scene by Raymond Gehman; sunset at Back Bay by Bill Portlock

A couple dances around the promenade of the Cavalier Beach Club in Virginia Beach.

BILL TIERNAN

PAUL SCHNABEL

Introduction

A mother, standing with her three children in the Jamestown Festival Park, gazed at three sailing ships docked at a pier, copies of the Susan Constant, the Godspeed, and the Discovery that brought the English settlers to Jamestown in 1607. "Look, children," she cried, pointing to the ships, "there are the three ships that brought the settlers here: the Nina, the Pinta and the Santa Maria!"

And now and then tourists come into the museum at Jamestown and, thinking of the Pilgrims, demand, "Where is the rock?" But anyway they are aware that something happened here. British historian A.L. Rowse put things in perspective. Looking out at the James River, he said, "Here is where it all began."

When the ships bearing 105 settlers hove onto the horizon, the Indians, sighting the white-winged vessels, must have had feelings we would experience in watching the landing of a spacecraft from Mars.

It was on April 26, 1607, after a violent storm, that the voyagers sighted land. A party of 20 ventured ashore. That night aboard ship, Captain Christopher Newport opened a chest that contained the Virginia Company's orders naming a governing council of nine. Luckily, one was Captain John Smith, a veteran soldier who arrived in the New World under arrest for his part in some shipboard dispute. The Company's instructions named him to the Council. The settlers later elected him president, and he saved the colony.

On April 29, they planted a wooden cross on a cape they named for Prince Henry. After beating about for two weeks, they moored upon a marshy, miasmic island in the river they named James and went ashore to start James Towne. They scarcely could have found a worse spot, but they clung to their toehold on the continent. Had they fled to England, as they tried to do once, the land would not long have remained unsettled. But failure at Jamestown would have meant a different America, with no Washington to command a fight for independence, no Henry to fire emotions, no Jefferson or Mason to define their rights, no Madison to fix them in a constitution. As it was, Jamestown, Williamsburg, and Yorktown formed a cradle for America: born in Jamestown, coming of age in Williamsburg, winning independence at Yorktown.

Hampton Roads, a vast offshoot of the Chesapeake Bay, is formed at the confluence of three rivers, the Nansemond, the Elizabeth, and the James. Seen from the air as it nears the Roads, the yawn-broad

The 100-ton Godspeed nestles by the 97,000-ton carrier Roosevelt at Newport News Shipbuilding.

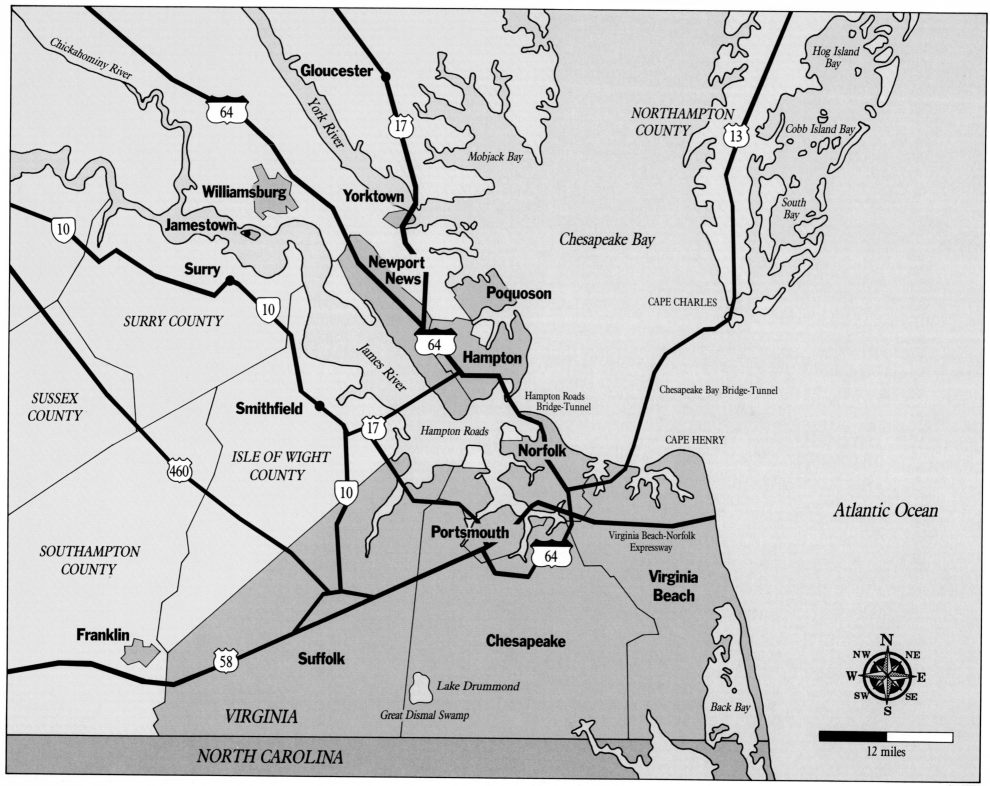

Chickahominy River

64

Williamsburg

Jamestown

10

Surry

SURRY COUNTY

SUSSEX
COUNTY

460

SOUTHAMPTON
COUNTY

Franklin

58

Gloucester

York River

17

Yorktown

Newport
News

10

James River

Smithfield

ISLE OF WIGHT
COUNTY

17

10

Hampton Roads

Suffolk

VIRGINIA

Mobjack Bay

64

Hampton

Poquoson

Hampton Roads
Bridge-Tunnel

Portsmouth

64

Chesapeake

Lake Drummond

Great Dismal Swamp

NORTH CAROLINA

NORTHAMPTON
COUNTY

13

Chesapeake Bay

CAPE CHARLES

Chesapeake Bay Bridge-Tunnel

CAPE HENRY

Norfolk

Virginia Beach-Norfolk
Expressway

Virginia
Beach

Back Bay

Hog Island
Bay

Cobb Island Bay

South
Bay

Atlantic Ocean

N
NW   NE
W   E
SW   SE
S

12 miles

8

BILL PITZER

Off the Eastern Shore, a sailboat finds its destination: serenity.

9

James moves with lazy loops across the flat land, turning back to see where it has been — an abiding trait of many Virginians as well as the river.

Insatiably curious John Smith, who wrote copiously of the region when it floated dugout canoes, would be fascinated with it today as it bears aircraft carriers displacing 97,000 tons. To many, the name Hampton Roads denotes the seven major cities around it, but this book brings in some neighbors. What distinguishes these sisters by the sea is their diversity. In the City of Norfolk is the world's largest naval base. Across the Roads, Newport News Shipbuilding has launched more than 700 ships in a century, including nuclear aircraft carriers with crews of 6,000, which only it can build. Newport News births 'em, Norfolk berths 'em. The City of Hampton has Langley Research Center, where astronauts learned to walk on the moon, and St. John's Episcopal Church, whose parishioners sip from the oldest communion cup in continuous use in the United States. Poquoson is a bedroom community of the families of watermen, scientists, shipbuilders, and aircraft pilots. Across the York River near Gloucester is the Virginia Institute of Marine Science working to keep the Chesapeake Bay alive.

On the south side of the James are Smithfield of the peerless ham, and the counties of Surry, site of Bacon's Castle; Isle of Wight with centuries-old St. Luke's Church; and Southampton, world champion producer of peanuts, adjoining the world's capital for manufacturing peanut products, the City of Suffolk. Chesapeake and Suffolk share the 150 square miles of the Great Dismal Swamp National Wildlife Refuge. At Chesapeake's Fentress Airfield, pilots from aircraft carriers practice landing on the outlines of flight decks painted on the runway. The Eastern Shore has barrier islands untouched by human habitation. Virginia Beach presents a lovely beach. Portsmouth offers Olde Towne, the largest clutch of 18th and 19th century dwellings between Alexandria, Va. and Charleston, S.C.

In Portsmouth, Norfolk, and Newport News there are skylines soaring 23 stories high that didn't exist 20 years ago — the giant cranes used to swing boxcar-sized containers between ship and shore. Seen across miles of water against an orange evening sky, they are gaunt monsters from Mars stalking across Hampton Roads. These structures at marine terminals in the three cities signify that the Port of Hampton Roads is the fastest growing in the United States.

Early Virginians, eyes turned westward, took the ports for granted, an attitude that persisted well into the 20th century. Cities on the fall line blocked any extension of railroads to Norfolk prior to the Civil War, and the General Assembly dumped $100,000 into building canals into the interior. In 1951, when North Carolina

Seashore State Park offers refuge to birds and beasts and a million human visitors annually, right.

10

was investing $7 million in ports, the Virginia General Assembly mustered $58,000. In 1952, a study commission led by Norfolk Del. James W. Roberts persuaded the legislators to confer independence on the Virginia State Port Authority, and Gov. John S. Battle raised the biennial appropriation to $350,000, which Roberts' colleagues hiked to $450,000. An area study, led by Hunter Phelan of Norfolk and Raymond B. Bottom of Newport News, supported Del. Roberts' findings. Succeeding governors increased the funds.

Things began to come together for the ports. Norfolk City Manager Thomas Maxwell learned in 1965 that the Maritime Administration had declared surplus a huge former Army terminal on the Elizabeth River. Maxwell sought to buy it for Norfolk. "I worked harder on that than any other project in my life," he said in 1987. One problem was that the Coast Guard wanted it. Maxwell asked Rep. Porter Hardy Jr. for help. "If it hadn't been for Porter there wouldn't have been any Norfolk International Terminal," Maxwell recalled. "He fought everybody in Washington to get it."

Maxwell and Hardy found in Portsmouth a site that the ever helpful Norfolk and Western Railway agreed to sell to satisfy the Coast Guard. Next, Hardy coaxed two federal agencies to release the old Army terminal, which was appraised at $17 million. Norfolk bought it for $6.5 million. "I just knew in my bones we ought to keep that land for the port," Maxwell said.

When the era of containers dawned, Norfolk had the property, and it had a leader in James N. Crumbley, who had been hired from New Orleans. Portsmouth Marine Terminals, led by C.B. Keowan and John T. Nix, followed Norfolk into developing container facilities. The two cities were on the heels of New York and several jumps ahead of other ports.

The cities' three terminals continued to compete among themselves, and Gov. Linwood Holton pushed the Virginia State Port Authority in 1971 into buying them. Even that did not diminish the strife. A study headed by Norfolk Sen. Edward L. Breeden Jr. advised the Port Authority in 1981 to bring the three ports into a single agency under one manager. The Port Authority created Virginia International Terminals and picked Crumbley to head it. Deregulation of railroads also helped. Freed from a rigid rate structure, the Norfolk Southern developed favorable rates for the three Virginia ports so that they could compete with rival Baltimore in reaching the Midwest. On the Peninsula, CSX cooperated with Newport News Marine Terminals on such special shipments as locomotives destined for China and steel imported for the automobile industry. Coal flows through Lamberts Point Coal Piers in Norfolk and two private piers in Newport News. Sewells Point Pier in Norfolk handles break-bulk cargo. The Port of Hampton Roads gained an edge when Richard N.

A young black bear, one of 250 of its kind in the Dismal Swamp, is upward bound, at left.

Below, a steam locomotive at West Ghent Terminal of Norfolk Southern, offers excursions into the past.

BILL KELLEY III

ARTHUR POLIZOS ASSOCIATES

Above, beaded patterns of coal cars may be seen at Lamberts Point in Norfolk or at three private piers in Newport News. Stacked containers at the Norfolk International Terminal appear to be a Grand Canyon of colors, right.

SCOTT KINGSLEY

12

Longshoremen appear to be doing a Zorba-like dance as they direct a tug pushing a ship to dock, at left.

At left, containership and longshoremen wait under a crane at the Norfolk International Terminal. A crane unloads a locomotive from a ship dock-side at the Newport News terminal, above.

Knapp, engineering director at VIT, invented a high-speed double-hoist crane that works twice as fast as its predecessor. VIT bought three in 1987, part of a $33 million project aimed at putting the terminals 30 years ahead of any ships on the drawing board. In 1986, Hampton Roads directed the flow of traffic for an annual foreign trade valued at $12 billion and creating 114,000 jobs with tax revenues in excess of $300 million annually. Hampton Roads often ranks first in foreign trade tonnage. In 1986-87, 15 new steamship lines began calling here.

Other port activities include a research service operated by Old Dominion University, the Virginia Center of World Trade. Promoting international trade, it develops and conducts seminars, training programs, and research activities for corporate and government leaders. Another port activity, the Virginia Export Trading Company, helps involve small and medium-sized firms with international trade and increase general cargo tonnage at Hampton Roads. In 1986, the General Assembly, funding Gov. Gerald L. Baliles' massive transportation program, earmarked $20 million yearly for ports.

There is scarcely any day in the year when a feast isn't taking place in Hampton Roads. A person could thrive simply by going from feast to feast. And one good fest begets another. In the woods at Wakefield in early May, when shad and politicians begin to run, there is a shad-planking. While the shad, split open and nailed to a plank, bake to a golden turn over a trench of hot coals, some 3,000 men sip drinks, listen to speeches, and tell stories. The din sounds as if a flock of starlings has lit in the grove. Leaving the planking one season, a band of Chincoteaguers resolved to hold their own spring seafood festival, the first requirement being that politicians could attend but they could not make speeches. In Virginia Beach, Tabernacle United Methodist Church holds an annual Lotus Festival although the lotus have long since left. Meeting and eating go on.

In 1987, Smithfield inaugurated a festival celebrating products from the largest packinghouses on the East Coast. The long-shank Smithfield ham, at least nine months in curing, is the Stradivarius of hams. The longer it cures, the sweeter it sings. And as the carver wields his knife, starting at the small end, working upward, twirling the knife, wafting slices that are well nigh veil thin, it is as if he is at work with his bow on the Strad. With ample farm land in Virginia Beach, Chesapeake, Suffolk, and Poquoson, Hampton Roads is a movable feast. By looking in such places as Bennett's Creek Farms, Williams, Bergey's, Oliver's Farm Market, or Billy's Produce, one may eat October tomatoes. At

Quiet barns amid a green and yellow setting speak of pastoral peace at Bayville Farms in Virginia Beach, above. Hampton Roads abounds in produce stands, such as Shorty's in Suffolk, at right.

JOHN H. SHEALLY II

MICHELE McDONALD

CATHY DIXON

Virginia Beach Farmers Market, following peaches with a truck from South Carolina to Pennsylvania, Cowboy and Brenda Modlin extend the season.

In December 1916, looking for a place near Washington with a mild climate and close to water, the federal government bought farms near the Back River for an aviation experimental station. Construction began in July 1917 and the next month the station was named Langley Field for aviation's Samuel Pierpont Langley. It became the Langley Research Center in 1958 when the National Aeronautics and Space Administration supplanted the National Advisory Committee for Aeronautics. Langley has been the fountainhead for both NACA and NASA. Between 1941 and 1944, Langley worked as a trouble-shooting lab for the military, helping, Navy Secretary Frank Knox said, to break Japan's grip in the Pacific. Research under way at Langley also made it possible for NASA to launch plans for manned spaceflight in Project Mercury. Langley personnel formed the Special Task Force that managed the Mercury Program and in 1962 established the NASA Manned Space Craft Center at Houston, Texas, while Lyndon Johnson was president. (Langley and Norfolk had been among other proposed sites.)

At Langley, the astronauts prepared to walk in the moon's gravitational field. Dressed in spacesuits harnessed in slings, cables, and the trolley of a simulator, they looked like children suited up for a cold day. Their walker was the Lunar Landing Research Facility, a gleaming silver and red structure reared against the sky, as if built from a child's Erector set, a steel gantry 250 feet high and 400 feet long. A manned rocket-powered research vehicle, a four-legged disk-footed contraption, dropped on a line from the top of the gantry looked like something dreamed up by Dr. Seuss. The lunar lander's floor was like the moon's terrain.

While training for the Mercury program, the astronauts lived in Hampton and Virginia Beach. The Hampton City Council named seven bridges for them. When they all had been recognized, a councilman sighed, "Thank the Lord, I thought we were going to have to build another bridge!"

Also looming on Langley's horizon are five huge vacuum spheres for storing compressed air to power wind tunnels, silver cocoons from which are spun solutions to problems posed by high-speed flights. About two-thirds of Langley's research focuses on aeronautics, the remainder on space. Its 190 buildings on 600 acres are worth $1.5 billion. Its employees total more than 5,500. Its future is bright. It will help design a space station to orbit the earth in the 1990s; do research for voyages to other planets; experiment on commercial

Far left: On the Eastern Shore, greens find their way in a basket on their way to the bread basket. At left, John Williams and his grandson, Johnny, are among four generations on the Williams Farm in Virginia Beach.

airplanes that travel five times the speed of sound and military planes 12 times as fast as sound; help design computers to control airplanes and robots to repair satellites. Generating ideas, Langley Research Center is peering 20 years into the future.

During a summer arts festival in Norfolk, a local production of "Cosi Fan Tutti" was so acclaimed that musicians asked Edie Harrison, a civic organizer, to lead in forming an opera company. She insisted that it would have to be a first-rate professional company. Even her husband doubted she could do it. "If you're lucky," Stanley Harrison said, "you'll sell 12 tickets. No, I take that back. Make that 11. I'm not coming."

But she gathered a board of fervent opera buffs, eager to work, found at the University of California a gifted conductor, Peter Mark, who recruits casts of fine singers, especially those upward bound. In 1975, hundreds had to be turned away at the box office for the first offering, "La Boheme." In the audience for the second, "La Traviata," was Andrew Porter, the New Yorker magazine's critic. Edie Harrison took his warm review, "Violetta in Virginia," with her to raise funds.

The board expanded to encompass all of Hampton Roads, started programs in the schools, opened a season in Richmond, and toured Virginia as far as Big Stone Gap. Those taking part included persons from every walk of life. And what about Stanley Harrison? "He loved it," she said. "Not only did he come to every production, he came to every single performance — and he would stand in the aisle because I sold his seat."

Under Music Director Winston Dan Vogel, the Virginia Symphony enjoyed a 20 percent boost in subscriptions. It presents more than 100 concerts, including a pops series in Norfolk, Virginia Beach, and Hampton under Skitch Henderson. It reaches 16,000 schoolchildren through young people's concerts. The Virginia Beach Pops, directed by Walter Noona, presents eight pairs of concerts at the Virginia Beach Pavilion. The Virginia Stage Company, a regional professional theater, performs in a magnificent Beaux Arts building, the renovated Wells Theatre in Norfolk. The Generic Theatre surprises audiences with experimental plays. The Tidewater Dinner Theatre flourishes as do Little Theatres in Norfolk, Portsmouth, Virginia Beach, Franklin, and Smithfield. The Williamsburg Players offer a wide variety, and the Peninsula Community Theatre specializes in musicals.

At the Norfolk Naval Base, the world's largest military complex, 110,000 sailors and Marines serve on 127 ships, in 59 aircraft squadrons, in 83 other fleet

Amid geysers of balloons, Newport News Shipbuilding launches a submarine named for the City of Newport News, right. Facing page: White-clad sailors line the decks, including the mountainous island of the battleship Iowa at the Norfolk Naval Base.

MARK

At left, two couples depart happily from the Naval Base pier. Facing page: Just returned to Oceana Naval Air Station from Libyan operations in April 1986, a fighter pilot of Attack Squadron 55 has eyes only for his wife.

MICHELE McDONALD

RAYMOND GEHMAN

At left, sailors and their families gather for a reunion on a pier at the Norfolk Naval Base. Above, husband and wife embrace on a pier at the Norfolk Naval Base, oblivious, but only momentarily, of the child at their feet.

JOHN H. SHEALLY II

19

commands and units and with 79 shore activities. NATO's Supreme Allied Commander Atlantic is in Norfolk, the only NATO command on U.S. soil. At Fort Story, the 79th Transportation Battalion maintains the Army's Lighter Air Cushion Vehicle. The Navy bases aircraft at Oceana Naval Air Station in Virginia Beach and the Norfolk Naval Air Station. At Dam Neck is the Navy's Fleet Combat Training Center. Portsmouth has the 5th District of the Coast Guard. On the Peninsula are the Army Transportation Center at Fort Eustis, the Tactical Air Command Headquarters at Langley Air Force Base and the Training and Doctrine Command at Fort Monroe.

Military personnel put down roots quickly, because, on a moment's notice, they may be planted elsewhere. They have the air of being able to function gracefully in any situation. The new to them is the status quo. A moving sight is that of reunions beside a warship. As it inches toward shore, those on deck and dock strain to see each other. The ties between them having extended across oceans, never parting, "like gold to airy thinness beat," are now pulling them together. If it's a carrier what seems at first a white tasseled fringe around its cliff-like edges becomes the men standing on the rim looking for loved ones below. When it is docked at last, the crowd screams, holds up signs, blows kisses. Then the men are racing down gangplanks, like waters pouring, until, in a torrent of emotion, families are in each other's arms, crying, laughing. They turn together toward home, the tides of love draining away to other parts of the city and, gradually, to other cities and towns, and isolated houses across the country, while the great gray ship sits quietly, waiting.

In July 1987, Patrick Peterson of the Newport News Daily Press figured that $75 million was being invested on 20 cultural attractions in Hampton Roads. The Mariners' Museum will spend $3 million for a 23,000-square-foot addition including space to house remnants of the ironclad Monitor that will be retrieved off Hatteras where it sank in a storm after its historic bout with the CSS Virginia (Merrimack). The Peninsula Fine Arts Center is spending $1.25 million to triple gallery space. An addition to the War Memorial Museum of 6,000 square feet will cost $575,000. The Jamestown Festival Park will double display space to 30,000 square feet at $3 million. For $1.35 million the Muscarelle Museum of Art at William and Mary College will double its size. The Abby Aldrich Rockefeller Folk Art Center at Wiliamsburg is undergoing a $5 million expansion. The Waterman's Museum at Yorktown has

Waiting to call home, sailors at telephones are a familiar sight on the Norfolk Naval Base when the fleet arrives, above. In the final act of commissioning the submarine Honolulu, the men run aboard and line up along the hull, left. Facing page: The battleship Iowa's teak deck takes on a rosy hue under Christmas lighting.

Something engrosses children peering into an exhibit at the Virginia Living Museum in Newport News, above. In the Virginia Zoological Park in Norfolk, three friends share a quiet moment, right. Far right: A beaver, oblivious to spectators, goes about his business in an environmental setting at the Virginia Living Museum.

22

Wave-like decor accents the long, low-slung building housing the Virginia Marine Science Museum, above. At left, visitors to the Virginia Marine Science Museum gather along the 125-foot aquarium of specimens from the Chesapeake Bay.

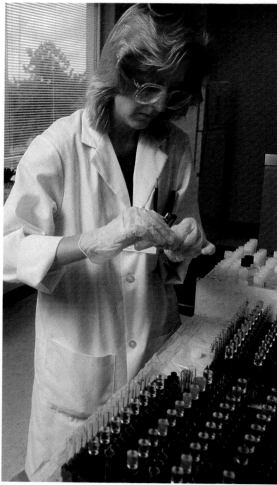

MICHELE McDONALD (2)

In the Eastern Virginia Medical School of the Medical College of Hampton Roads, a technician works in the laboratory, above.

moved into Cypress Manor, which was floated across the York River. At the Yorktown Victory Center, an 18th century working farm is being added. In Hampton's downtown, the Virginia Air and Space Center and Hampton Roads History Center will cost $20 million for an 80,000-square-foot complex including theater and NASA Visitors Center.

In South Hampton Roads, the Suffolk Museum will use $18,000 to renovate an old library into a museum. Norfolk's Hermitage Museum, a 12-acre oasis, received a gentle refurbishing. A new Portsmouth museum, costing $8 million, probably will include the Naval Shipyard Museum. The new 32,000-square-foot Virginia Beach Arts Center will cost $5.2 million.

A campaign for $10.5 million enabled the Chrysler Museum in Norfolk to double its space to 150,000 square feet and draw from its permanent collection to display art from every major culture. In downtown Norfolk, the d'Art Center used $550,000 to renovate a building with studios for 40 artists. Norfolk is looking to build a $37.4 million National Maritime Center near Waterside celebrating the sea and the seagoing.

In a speech to a civic club in 1958, the executive director of the Norfolk Redevelopment and Housing Authority, Lawrence M. Cox, suggested that the region's newly created medical center should have a medical school. The idea caught on, and after being studied twice, it won the General Assembly's approval. Dr. Mason C. Andrews, president of the Medical Center Authority, and Charles L. Kaufman, the Housing Authority chairman, persuaded Porter Hardy Jr. to lead the campaign that raised $15 million. Norfolk's City Council gives more than $600,000 annually. Other localities bring the sum to $1 million. Eastern Virginia Medical School affiliated with 31 hospitals from the Eastern Shore to Franklin, and it lifted the area's level of medical care. It drew world attention with the birth of the nation's first "test-tube" baby, which was conceived at its Howard and Georgeanna Jones Institute for Reproductive Medicine, the most comprehensive fertility center in the country. And the medical school reaches out to the world when Drs. Charles E. Horton and Charles J. Devine Jr. recruit teams to do plastic reconstructive surgery in underdeveloped countries.

In offering courses at 50 sites through Hampton Roads, Old Dominion University works to fill a regional role. In a poll of 800 college presidents, U.S. News & World Report ranked it among the 10 top comprehensive universities in the Southeast. It offers a dozen doctoral, 47 master's, and 78 bachelor's degree programs. Its oceanography program has built an international reputation. Its programs in computer science and education are the largest in Virginia, and its psychology program is one of the best in the Southeast.

Contributing to the region's intellectual ferment are community colleges in Virginia Beach, Portsmouth, Chesapeake, Hampton, and Franklin. CBN University

offers a wide range of graduate-level programs, including the CBN School of Law. Students in its communications school have produced a movie that won an Emmy. Christopher Newport College in Newport News offers seven degrees in more than 30 majors. Hampton University has master's degrees in several disciplines and a curriculum that ranges from architecture to media art. Norfolk State University offers master's degrees, and its education courses include an outstanding one in gifted children. Virginia Wesleyan College offers intensive study in liberal arts for a relatively small student body. As for the College of William and Mary in Williamsburg, it has an outstanding law school and bills itself, rightly, as "alma mater to the nation."

Hampton Roads abounds in historic structures. The Moses Myers House in Norfolk was home to merchant Moses and Eliza and their descendants until the 1930s. His portrait by Gilbert Stuart is on the wall, and you feel that, at a turn, you might meet the subject. In 1635, Captain Adam Thoroughgood was granted 5,300 acres on the Lynnhaven River by Charles I's Privy Council for bringing his family and 105 other persons to settle there. A descendant probably built the house. In the chimney's mortar a dog left a paw print to posterity. When Norfolk burned in the Revolution, only Old St. Paul's walls were left standing. They also survived urban renewal. Scientific analysis disclosed that the Lynnhaven House in Virginia Beach was built about 1725. It lost 40 years but the revelation of the owner's name, Francis Thelaball, enabled curators to recall its environment. The thick-walled brick house shows that there were solid houses between the James River plantations and cabins.

There are solid instances of cooperation among the communities of Hampton Roads. When tolls were lifted from the Hampton Roads Bridge Tunnel in 1976, civic leaders recognized the importance of joining the two sides of Hampton Roads into one metropolitan market. The movement vaulted the region into 28th place among major metropolitan markets.

Working through the Southeastern Public Service Authority, eight south-side communities joined to build a waste-disposal plant. In disposing of the communities' solid waste, it derives fuel that it sells to the Norfolk Naval Shipyard. "We take something normally useless and make something beneficial of it," said Durwood S. Curling, the authority's executive director.

In 1982, area-wide civic leaders formed a goal-setting organization, the Future of Hampton Roads. "There are so many things that we can do well collectively that we'll do badly as rivals," said Henry Clay Hofheimer II, its president. Five years later, the group's executive vice president, retired Adm. Harry D. Train II, remarked that good has come from the communities' meeting regularly to talk about problems and opportunities. From one such discussion this book grew.

At left, the band at Hampton University practices its routines. A teacher's intensity holds her students at Virginia Wesleyan College, below.

Middle: Academic procession at Christopher Newport College proceeds at a stroll. Bottom: A cameraman films a scene for CBN University.

Top row, left to right: The Moses Myers House, an elegant 18th century townhouse, features original furnishings. Old St. Paul's Church, gutted by fire during the Revolutionary War, survives amid urban renewal. The ancient Adam Thoroughgood House sits serenely amid modern homes in Virginia Beach.

Far left: In Suffolk, Riddick's Folly is serving a most useful function as a multi-purpose museum. The sturdy Lynnhaven House stands midway between the river plantations and the log cabins in Colonial Virginia. Facing page: St. John's Church, the oldest structure in the City of Hampton, survives wars and time.

Hampton's parade, celebrating its 350th birthday in 1985, features a green frog with attendant youths, right.

KENNETH STUTZ

Mr. Peanut, symbol of Suffolk's supremacy in manufacturing peanut products, greets onlookers during the annual Peanut Fest, right. During Liberty Sail '86, a tall ship with men in its yardarms enlivens Portsmouth's waterfront, above.

Even the ocean fails to distract spectators at the Boardwalk Art Show in Virginia Beach, left.

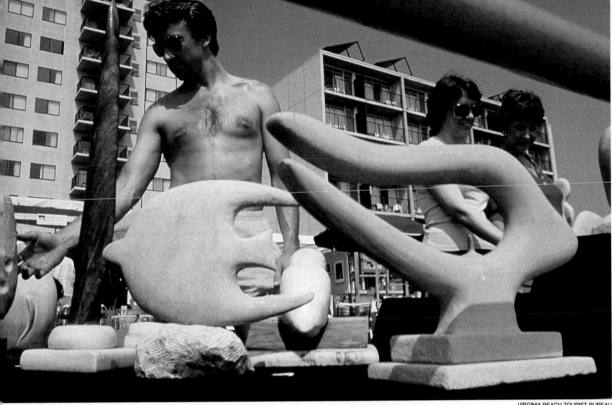

Above, Louisa Venable Kyle, author of "The Witch of Pungo," brightens the prospect at the annual Pungo Strawberry Festival. At left, Ringling's Gunther Gabel-Williams and his elephants salute the world outside the Hampton Coliseum.

MICHELE McDONALD

Historic Triangle

Jamestown, where we started, presents the ruins of the ivy-covered Old Church Tower, part of the first brick church built in 1639, the only standing remains of the settlement. Entering the Old Tower, you step across the sill of time. The square, deep ruin, open to the stars and the trees' traceries, is flooded with mellow gloom as if the light is sifting down through centuries.

Attached to the Tower is the Memorial Church, built in 1907 by the Colonial Dames of America. In the floor along one wall is a glass-covered trench exposing the most ancient evidence of all: the gray cobblestone base of the first wood church. It is also the foundation of the United States Congress and the statehouses, for in that church on July 30, 1619, was the convening of the Council and the elected House of Burgesses, the nation's first legislative body. Its 27 members met in the "quire" and adopted, among other things, a law fixing the price of tobacco.

On Jamestown's shore, looking westward, is a statue of stocky Capt. John Smith, his right hand on his sword. Without him and one more, England's little colony would never have survived its toehold on the continent. Half the company were gentlemen and gallants, most of them "roarers and loiterers," Smith said. Putting them to work ("He that will not worke shall not eate"), pouring a dipper of cold water down their sleeves when they shirked, trading with the Indians and learning their language, waging a careful cold war with the redman's Emperor Powhatan, exploring the enticing rivers to the interior, mapping it all, he was carrying out the Virginia Company's orders, but he was doing it, really, for John Smith, eager to see what marvel the next bend of the river or hilltop disclosed. He scorned those around Jamestown who "never adventured to know anything."

After two years, an accidental gunpowder explosion forced his return to England. He relived every adventure, writing about it, and giving his maps to those who would settle New England. His accounts show him to be one who loved America, not for the gold he called fool's glitter, but for herself in all her incredible diversity. In a way he was the first American, prophesying a new society that, with abundant resources, could give each individual a chance to be his or her best self.

And of all that he beheld, nothing matched in won-

Where cannon roared on the battlefield at Yorktown in October 1781, children scamper.

33

Clad in colonial costumes, Virginians reenact settlers venturing ashore in the New World, right. Below, a statue of Pocahontas, arms open in welcome, her role in life.

At right, three ships, typifying those that brought the colonists, await tourists at Jamestown. Far right: Ruins of the Old Church Tower of 1639 dominate Jamestown. Facing page: Capt. John Smith's statue looks to the horizon, as he did.

der or importance a girl of 11, Pocahontas. When the captive John Smith, his head on a stone, was about to be executed, she threw her arms around him and pleaded for his life with her father, Powhatan. Nor was that the first time she saved Smith and the Colony. She slipped through the woods to warn the English of attacks by her father's braves and repeatedly brought food to the palisade. As long as she lived, the two races were at peace.

In 1613, the colonists held her hostage. With her gift for making the best of any circumstance, she lived among them cheerfully, named Rebecca after being baptized, and married John Rolfe. In 1616, the couple went with Gov. Dale and a dozen Indians to England. Having crossed from the stone age to life in Jamestown, she made another transition to the Court of St. James. When John Smith came to see her, nearly 10 years after she had saved his life, she was so moved that he left her alone a while. When he returned, Pocahontas reminded him that he had promised Powhatan that "what was yours would be his, and he the like to you; you called him father, being in his land a stranger. And by the same reason, so must I do you."

She brushed aside Smith's protest that she, a king's daughter, should not call him father. Had he not, she asked, come into her father's country "and caused feare in him and all of his people and feare you here I should call you father? I tell you I will, and you shall call me child, and so I will be for ever and ever your Countrieman."

In 1617, Rolfe boarded ship with his family to return to Jamestown, but off Gravesend, Pocahontas fell ill. Accepting death with the serenity with which she had greeted all the turns in her short life, she told her husband, "All must die. It is enough the child liveth."

The child did, and through him, thousands. The child that was the Colony also prospered and became a Country, although in dealing with her people, it failed to follow her compassionate example.

"For ever and ever your Countrieman" comes to us through the centuries, a reproach, a reminder, a summary of the way of a Virginian who tried to reconcile races and cultures.

"The mother of us all," poet Vachel Lindsay called her.

"Poor little maid," Smith wrote. "I sorrowed much for her thus early death, and even now cannot think of it without grief, for I felt toward her as if she were mine own daughter." That she was in love with him never seems to have occurred to the ordinarily perceptive little Captain.

Near the Old Church Tower is a statue of Pocahontas coming out of the wilderness, opening and raising her arms, the hands palm out, as if in a moment she will break into a run in her eagerness to greet those she loves. The settlers, peering out of the palisade, saw her approaching thus so many times as to seem a part of the landscape, as she is now.

In 1699, the legislators, who had been burned out of their fourth statehouse, gave up miasmic Jamestown and moved the Capitol six miles inland to the Middle Plantation, which they named Williamsburg, honoring King William II. It became the seedbed for leaders of the American Revolution. From there, George Washington went to fight in the French and Indian War; Patrick Henry raised his voice as the bugle of independence; John Marshall learned law from George Wythe; and a 16-year-old redhead, Thomas Jefferson, found at the College of William and Mary the teachers who inspired him to become the da Vinci of the American renaissance of government. There were others.

Then, having fathered a country, Williamsburg slept. So soundly that in 1912 it forgot to hold an election. Nobody remembered to open the polls in the town where Patrick Henry had crowed defiance of the Crown and heralded the Republic's daybreak. In 1913, rather than pay $50 to have the town clock cleaned and wound, the City Council let it run down. Time stopped. Until one evening, after a Phi Beta Kappa dinner at William and Mary, the Rev. W.A.R. Goodwin, rector of Bruton Parish Church, walked with John D. Rockefeller Jr. along the dilapidated streets and suggested that he resurrect an entire town. Shortly thereafter Williamsburg began to stir as Dr. Goodwin began acquiring property for the great restoration. Jack Hundley rimed the rumors that swept the town:

My gawd, they've sold the town,
They've sold the whole damn town.
And it is said the news has spread
For many miles around.

They've sold the courthouse green,
I daresay, all the people,
They'll sell the church, the vestry too
And even sell the steeple.

They've sold the Powder Horn,
The School House and the lawn.
It is the tale they've sold the jail
And the streets we walk upon.

It is a sacrilege
The way they trade and barter.
Next they'll sell Botetourt
And then our Alma Mater.

The streets will all come up
And the poles will all go down
Take my word, oh Stranger,
It's going to be some town.

And it did. In 1926, work began on restoring some 90 buildings and 100 acres of gardens. Rockefeller's insistence on authenticity never slipped nor did the Restoration's standards for excellence. What a relief it is

for Virginians to say, when company comes, "Oh, let's go to Williamsburg!" — knowing that guides, films, and the buildings themselves save a lot of explaining about the Revolution and all that. The State Department caught the habit of letting Williamsburg speak for America. It whisks foreign dignitaries by helicopter to the Capitol for a day or two of restoration before entering 20th century D.C.

History arranged, conveniently, that the American Revolution ended at Yorktown only a 15-minute drive from Williamsburg. Two information centers are on the battlefield — state-sponsored Victory Center and federally funded Visitors Center — and scarcely a week passes but what a wild-eyed tourist shows up at one center to report that his car has been stolen when, all the time, it is at the other center where he parked it. The British couldn't have picked a more beautiful field on which to lose an empire. On a grassy bluff 50 feet above the York River, it seems more fit for a picnic than a battle. It rings with the song of mockingbirds. Nothing else in American history illustrates better than Yorktown the virtue of hanging on. Most of the war George Washington maneuvered to keep his tiny army from engaging the vastly superior British forces. Often, all the Americans had was Washington. In Yorktown, you come bang upon his staff tent, pitched as it was in the field, and that patch of canvas was the mobile headquarters for a new, often faltering nation. His character was the sustaining force when the seasonal army of three-month enlistments dwindled to 1,500 men. A French emissary, sent to size up the situation, reported that it didn't matter how many battles the Americans lost, as long as they had George Washington they would win the war. He seemed immune to bullets. When his men were being routed at Monmouth, Washington was suddenly in their midst in his blue and buff uniform, astride his white charger, as if he were a demigod dropped from the clouds, rallying them. A major said he covered his eyes with his hat so as not to see his leader fall. The men regrouped and saved the day.

In April 1782, Washington wrote to Gen. Lafayette that "it may be declared in a word that we are at the end of our tether, and that now or never our deliverance must come." It came suddenly in October. British Gen. Cornwallis, having harried his way through the Carolinas and chased through Virginia "that boy" Lafayette, paused in Portsmouth and then marched to Yorktown, where he expected reenforcements from Gen. Henry Clinton, then in New York.

Thanks to the French, who had sent a chest of gold, soldiers under Gen. Rochambeau, and ships under doughty Adm. De Grasse, Washington, for the first time, had a force superior to the British. He slipped away from New York, met the French, and dug in with

Bright-clad Drum and Fife Corps vies with Williamsburg's fall foliage, left.

MICHELE McDONALD

16,000 men before Yorktown where Cornwallis had 9,000. De Grasse's French ships from the West Indies fought the English fleet to a draw at the mouth of the Chesapeake Bay and thereby cut off Cornwallis from help by sea.

When the Allies' cannonading was about to begin, Gen. Lafayette asked where in Yorktown Cornwallis might have his headquarters. Thomas Nelson, Governor of Virginia and commander of the militia, pointed to his own impressive house. There, he said, was where his lordship would most likely be. Then he turned his horse and rode away. During the war he paid for supplies for the army. After the war he paid his British creditors. In the graveyard of Grace Church an inscription on Nelson's tomb reads: He Gave All for Liberty.

The climax of the three-week siege was the Allies' assault on two outlying redoubts. Lt. Col. Alexander Hamilton, Washington's secretary and confidant, led a bayonet charge that cleared Redoubt 10 in 10 minutes and the French stormed Redoubt 9 in half an hour. At his place near the front lines, Washington said: "The work is done and well done. . . ."

Gloucester is tied to the triangle by the York River Bridge. Its old courthouse complex — an oasis of trees and half a dozen faded pink buildings dating to the 17th and 18th centuries — sits squarely in the middle of the road.

Really it is a walled circle within a square. Motorists swirl in cars on the one-way two-lane road around the circle, past quaint storefronts on their right while, on their left, the six pink buildings sit within a brick wall, under great trees, as if moated in time from the traffic. It seems enchanted ground. One steps within the circle, as if entering a charmed, tree-shaded island around which cars race.

A visitor might have the luck of finding, in the circle within the square, John Warren Cooke, editor of the Gazette-Journal and the last son of a Confederate veteran to serve in the General Assembly. His father, Giles B. Cooke, rode from Appomattox with Robert E. Lee. John Warren rose through the conservative Byrd Democratic Organization to become Speaker of the House of Delegates, where he exercised power in a fair, enlightened way. Like his father, who after the war became a clergyman and founded a school for black children in Petersburg, John Warren was aware of the underdog. He worked a quiet revolution by appointing blacks, women, liberals, and Republicans to the House's major committees, bringing them out of cold from committees that seldom, if ever, met.

"They had constituencies to represent," he said. "Those constituencies had to be heard." It was as plain to him as a geometric theorem. He is unfailingly courteous. Frequent "suhs" lace his talk. He gives his best "regyards" to a caller and says he will be looking "fareward" to seeing him again. The man and the circle within the square are compatible.

Among militia on review, one walls eyes heavenward, above. Far right: Circle in the square at Gloucester offers green oasis amid traffic. Thomas Nelson Jr.'s house, now at peace, suffered bombardment during Yorktown's siege, right. Facing page: In reenactment at Williamsburg, artillerists fire cannon during Fourth of July fanfare.

ANN MYERS

ROBIE RAY

Hampton

You're in the City of Hampton when, driving east on Interstate 64 toward Norfolk, you see looming on the left a great white ring of a building appealing to the eye: Hampton Coliseum, emblematic of the city's pluck.

Just before you come abreast of the Coliseum, the interstate takes you over Mercury Boulevard, named for NASA's Mercury program, which began a journey to the stars at Langley Research Center. The eight-lane nine-mile boulevard, lined with commerce, extends west into Newport News, which stretches 26 miles along the James River.

A little beyond the Coliseum, a lovely vignette opens. To the west is the Hampton River, specked with boats with handkerchief-sized sails. Townhouses line its bank. Behind them, rising nine stories in bold lines is the multi-ledged City Hall. Nearby are the Radisson Hotel and Harbor Centre, an office tower banded blue and red. In the scene's middle ground is a low-slung gleaming white bridge, gently curving as an eyelash, crossing the blue river. That quick scene in white, green, and blue outlines downtown Hampton.

The bridge, named for Booker T. Washington, connects downtown with Hampton University, from which the black leader proceeded in 1881 to found Tuskegee Institute in Alabama.

Off an exit on the interstate's east side is the village of Phoebus, its two main streets lined with storefronts from the late 19th and early 20th centuries. From Phoebus, a crooked road and a causeway cross an inlet to Fort Monroe, guarded by a seven-sided moat. During the Civil War, Confederates never tried to capture Fort Monroe because, some Southerners insist, there was no use trying; it had been engineered by Lt. Robert E. Lee when he was second in command there from 1831 until 1834. The facts are less consoling. A former aide to Napoleon, Simon Bernard, designed the Fort; Lee supervised its completion.

The core of Fort Monroe's Casemate Museum is the cell in which Jefferson Davis, former president of the Confederacy, was confined after he was captured in May 1865 in Irwinville, Ga. Charged with treason, Davis was guarded by soldiers around the clock. Its spare furnishings included an oil lamp, always lit. In October Davis was transferred to the Fort's officers quarters. Released in 1867, he was never brought to trial. Around the Fort they tell of a Southern grande dame who, arriving for a visit to the Jefferson Davis Casemate, praised the Fort's Georgia stonework. Told it was from

From Old Point Comfort in Hampton, spectators watch the USS America enter Hampton Roads.

BILL KELLEY III

Langley tests this joint as a building block for space stations, left. Facing page: Workmen install sky-blue panels in towering, rose-colored Harbor Centre in downtown Hampton.

Above, a 50-foot space antenna opens umbrella style to tower over scientists. From wind tunnels at Langley Research Center are spun solutions that permit airplanes to travel 12 times the speed of sound, at left.

Pennsylvania and that the Fort was a U.S. Army installation, she declared, "I'm not interested in seeing any ol' federal fort!" — and marched away.

On the approach road of the Hampton Roads Bridge Tunnel, looking east, the traveler sees a row of dwellings on Fort Monroe, reduced by the distance across the water to sentry boxes, and the Chamberlin Hotel on Old Point Comfort. The nine-story Chamberlin is a reviewing stand for ships moving through Hampton Roads. The squarish old hotel, when its lines are stark at midday or when the walls of weathered red brick are bathed in the rays of the setting sun, seems impervious to time, as if encased in an oval paperweight.

Fort Monroe houses 17 Army installations of the Training and Doctrine Command. Most picturesque is the U.S. Continental Army Band. Another is the Coast Guard's Old Point Comfort Light Station. After a hurricane destroyed the fort in 1749, a lone caretaker, bored, put a light on the point to guide ships. It stayed.

Old Point Comfort entered history after Capt. Christopher Newport guided the first successful settlers to a landing on Virginia's shores. After they went ashore and built a cross at what is now Cape Henry in Virginia Beach, he dispatched exploring parties. On April 30, 1607, a group rowed to a point where it found a channel, sounded 12 fathoms, and named it Cape Comfort. They saw Indians running on the shore and visited the village of Kicotan, easier to spell than Kecoughtan, as it is now. Two years later, on Oct. 3, 1609, Capt. James Davis arrived from England with 16 men in the pinnace Virginia. Under the guidance of Capt. John Radcliffe, these men, aided by a detachment from Jamestown, built a fort at Point Comfort. The old fort had its ups and downs, and it appears today as it did in its final guise just prior to the Civil War with a moat and walls 12 feet thick at the base, 12 feet in height.

Six years before the Civil War the five-story Chesapeake Female College arose on the shore of Hampton Roads. With the war's outbreak, the students fled. A Rebel began spying from the building, and Federal troops seized it and it became the Union's Chesapeake Military Hospital. After the war, when five military hospitals were to be built for veterans, Gen. Benjamin F. Butler, who had presided over the occupation of Norfolk, proposed that the former women's college be chosen because of the mild climate and proximity to black veterans. Butler owned the property, which he sold for $50,000.

Born amid war, the Veterans Administration Medical Center grew to its present size of 411 beds, an additional 400-bed domiciliary, and a 120-bed nursing home care unit. It has a staff of 1,250 employees and 300 volunteers.

The redevelopment of the downtown waterfront galvanized Hampton after World War II. The revival began when merchants asked Thomas P. Chisman, president of WVEC-TV, to advise them how to promote Christmas sales. Chisman enlarged the topic. Too many

MICHELE Mc

Above, students stroll along the waterfront of the Hampton River. An egret, perched atop a rail fence on the Hampton Golf Course, looks for a birdie, right. Facing page: Flags bedeck Victorian houses on Victoria Avenue.

44

KENNE

had failed to expand the businesses they had inherited, he said. The downtown was full of mostly empty warehouses.

"If we don't do something, we're going to be passed by," he warned, "and I know of but one solution: Tear it down and start over." The president thanked him and said someday, maybe, the merchants would do that. Alfred Goldstein arose to say he didn't think Chisman was talking about some day: "He's talking about now!" Bill Smith asked if he meant they should act promptly.

"Not only do I mean it," Chisman said, "I'll make the first contribution of $1,000 so we can plan what has to be done." The group raised $40,000 to hire planners for the redevelopment.

In 1959, a group of citizens asked civic leader Ann Kilgore to run for the City Council. With widespread support, she won. "Yesterday was Ladies Day," the Elks Club Bulletin observed. The day also proved a happy one for Hampton. Elected mayor two terms later, Mrs. Kilgore, an individual of high energy and humor, led an administration that promoted a dozen advances ranging from 50 kindergartens to the first public housing including a home for the elderly.

The building of Virginia's first coliseum symbolized Hampton's rejuvenation. It was to have been done by Hampton and Newport News but when a committee recommended a site in Hampton, Newport News withdrew. Hampton persisted and it opened at a cost of $8 million in 1969 — the buy of the year, said the American Institute of Architects. Rimmed by gigantic, high-pointed diamond-shaped panels like the sails in the nearby Hampton River, it looks to be a coronet or, at night, when the panels are flooded in lights, a setting of diamonds in a ring. When the circus is in town, elephants are tethered on an island in the Coliseum's lagoon. Motorists slow up at the sight of great beasts browsing by the huge structure. Not long after it was built, an excited taxpayer called Mrs. Kilgore at 7 a.m. "I want you to tell me the truth," he said. "Are there elephants, camels, and zebras on the island by the Coliseum?"

Redevelopment downtown produced Queensway Mall in Colonial architecture and a renovated waterfront by the Hampton Yacht Club, a forest of white spars. Along with the tidal flow of people, the downtown is thronged with thousands on such occasions as the annual Bay Days celebration each September. Enclaves of old Hampton persist. Victoria Boulevard, with lovely Victorian homes, is in the National Register of Historic Places. On that tree-lined street, American flags brighten deep porches. Putting out the flag has been a custom as long as he can remember, said Robert E. Long, whose great-grandfather built a house there. "I don't think it did have a beginning, to tell you the truth," he said. "It's just always been that way. The neighborhood is populated by patriotic people with ties to Newport News Shipbuilding, Fort Monroe, and Langley. They're not embarrassed by expressing support for their coun-

The Radisson Hotel is handy to the Visitors Center in downtown Hampton, above. At left, Hampton's many-ledged City Hall peeps above the rustic Mill Point condominiums at a passing sailboat. Facing page: Hampton Coliseum, lighted red, blue, and white in the night, offers a double visual treat for sightseers.

KEVIN McPARTLAND (2)

try. My grandmother had a flag flying while I was serving in Vietnam. It made me feel good to see it every time I came home."

Farther along Victoria is a magnificent public library of 53,000 square feet completed in 1986 at a cost of $4 million. It bespeaks Hampton's concern with education. The city has the nation's oldest continuous free schools. In 1634, Benjamin Syms left 200 acres and 8 cows in his will for a free school for the parish children. In 1659, surgeon Thomas Eaton left 500 acres and everything on them for a school.

Alongside the new library is the sizable old one, now used for the arts. Funds for its construction came from Mrs. Matthew Armstrong, whose husband was the nephew of Gen. Samuel Chapman Armstrong, Appointed chief of the Freedmen's Bureau during the Civil War, Armstrong understood how much former slaves yearned to learn. They gathered under the trees to recite ABCs. Armstrong inspired the American Missionary Association to contribute to founding Hampton Institute beside the river. Now a university, It opened in 1868 with Armstrong at its head.

One student who found his way there was Booker T. Washington, born in a slave cabin in Franklin County near Roanoke. Working in a West Virginia coal mine, the youth heard miners talking about "a great school for colored people somewhere in Virginia." He begged rides and walked 500 miles to Hampton Institute. A teacher, testing him, told him to sweep a room. He swept it three times, dusted it four times — woodwork, every bench, table, desk. Failing to find a speck of dirt, she said, "I guess you will do for this institution."

Hampton's oldest structure, St. John's Episcopal Church, is an oasis of greenery downtown. The parish began in 1610. The church, the fourth one in the parish, was built in 1728. It suffered damage during the Revolutionary War and the War of 1812 and was burned along with much of Hampton in the Civil War, but it survived. Its stained glass windows are storied. One shows Pocahontas being baptized in Jamestown. Plains Indians contributed to the window in return for what the church did for them while they were at Hampton Institute.

In 1903, the Association for the Preservation of Virginia Antiquities contributed a small window emblazoned with the names of the church's Colonial rectors. The rector of the day objected to the listing of Jeremiah Taylor, who began his ministry in 1667 and was often in court. The APVA declined to drop his name. As a compromise, Taylor's name was enclosed in brackets. Young women banded in the Bracket Club for tea dances in the Chamberlin. Tea dances are no more. The Bracket Club endures.

Hampton is a city with an eye to outer space. In December 1916, looking for a place near Washington with a mild climate, close to water, the federal government bought farms near the Back River for an "aviation experimental station and proving grounds." It grew into

47

Langley Research Center, pioneering through the universe.

And the City of Hampton, here on earth, is in fine shape, said Mayor James L. Eason. After a summer of civic stock-taking in 1982 and a yearlong party for Hampton's 375th anniversary in 1985, "our expectations as a community have risen," he said. The state of the economy is promising. "With NASA at one end and CEBAF (a $225 million atomic research machine) in Newport News at the other end, no other area in Virginia has two better anchors." Strengthened by the arrival in 1986 of a branch of Old Dominion University's engineering school, Hampton will be competing in research with California's Silicon Valley and North Carolina's Research Triangle, Eason predicted.

"We are spending as much time on quality of life as we are on the economy," he said. A museum of Hampton Roads history, to be built downtown, will also incorporate the NASA museum at the Langley Research Center, and the Syms-Eaton local museum. "The crown jewel of our downtown," Eason calls it. A sightseeing boat carries visitors to Fort Wool on an island in the Roadstead. It was a retreat for President Andrew Jackson.

To preserve five miles of beach for the public, the city bought the former Buckroe Amusement Park. Condominiums will be built on dredged material, but the wetlands of Grandview Beach will be preserved. The park's classic carousel will be redone and put downtown. The city moved to expand Blue Bird Park, a zoo of farm animals across from the Coliseum. A mile or two east of the Coliseum on Mercury Boulevard, the city planned an outdoor exhibit of aviation ranging from fixed-wing planes to jet and rocket planes.

City Manager Robert N. O'Neill noted the development of Hampton Roads Center, a premier office park up to 3 million square feet at Interstate 64 and four-lane Magruder Boulevard, including an extensive Health and Fitness Center, with golf course and lakes so that business people may step into links or lakes.

The city backs the Phoebus Improvement League, headed by Jack Shiver, to save that community's character against traffic pouring into it from I-64. "Phoebus still has a sense of community and identity second to none," O'Neill said, "and it can be preserved as a showplace of a business district of the late 19th or early 20th century."

Hampton, celebrating its 375th anniversary, unveiled a 15-foot statue by Barry Johnston. On the theme, "First from the sea, first to the stars," the bronze figure trails a fish net and points to the heavens. Given Hampton's go, he may be aiming to cast the net around the stars.

Barry Johnston's Spirit of Hampton trails a net and points to the stars, left. Facing page: White-clad sailors, gull-free, fast-stepping, parade for Hampton's 375th anniversary.

Newport News

In the 1980s, an increasing number of firms hunting for new sites began looking at Newport News, stretching 26 miles along the James River. Such was the surge of interest that Virginia Gov. Gerald L. Baliles likened the city of 156,000 to "an awakening giant."

"In so many ways that's apt," said Mayor Jessie M. Rattley. "A new day is dawning." Part of that new day is Mayor Rattley, the first woman and black to be chosen the city's Mayor. She was elected to the City Council in 1970 and won a fifth term in 1986 with the most votes ever cast.

"It's as if we in Newport News have just fully grasped our assets," she said. "Maybe they have been intensified by Interstate 664." Swinging southwest from Interstate 64 in Hampton, I-664 comes into downtown Newport News to the tunnel through which it will cross the James River and enter Suffolk, thereby completing a ring of interstate highways around the Roadstead. "Analyses of the traffic flow found that Newport News is an ideal location for business, and it must be so because we now have over $2 billion in projects," she said. She listed items ranging from $55 million for an Army distribution center to $236 million for the Continuous Electron Beam Accelerator Facility. CEBAF examines subatomic quarks through a 44-billion-volt accelerator that fires an electron beam to split the nucleus of an atom. The city plans to develop near CEBAF a 300-acre industrial park for high-technology research companies.

Previously, driving past woods on Interstate 64 in Newport News, travelers have been unaware that they were going through the city. "Motorists had to have a purpose to come here. Now, thanks to I-664, travelers to other places will come this way and stop and utilize our attractions," she said.

To promote unity, the Mayor and other Democrats on the Council, who had been expected to elect a Democrat as Vice Mayor, chose Republican Jerome Hogge Jr. He also characterized I-664 as a catalyst: "For the first time in our city's life, it has access to an interstate highway. Heretofore we couldn't get to one without going through Hampton."

A decade ago, during former Mayor Joseph C. Ritchie's administration, when it appeared that Newport News Shipbuilding might begin cutting employment, Hogge observed, Newport News and Hampton formed the Virginia Peninsula Economic Development Council and that led in 1984 to landing Canon USA at a site just off Interstate 64.

Among other inducements for new industry are ample water, the port, and a labor supply ranging from unskilled

Red, white, and blue balloons fill the sky as the USS Albany is launched at Newport News.

TOM BENNETT

workers to engineers, drawn there by the shipyard, he said. Joseph C. Biggins, the city manager for 40 years, began the quest for water by developing a reservoir that became the Newport News City Park. In the 1980s, the city added two reservoirs and is investing $54 million in expanding a treatment plant. It supplies water to neighboring communities, including 6 million gallons a day to Busch Gardens.

A congeries of museums also may lure travelers off Interstate 64. Near the entrance to Fort Eustis is the U.S. Army Transportation Museum. Inside are displays of 200 years of army transportation from the American Revolution to today; outside more than 50 vehicles, from Hovercraft to steam locomotives.

Exiting from I-64 exit onto J. Clyde Morris Boulevard will take the traveler to three museums, all clustered within about four blocks: the Virginia Living Museum, next to Riverside Hospital, and to the Peninsula Fine Arts Center and the Mariners Museum sharing a park at the intersection of J. Clyde Morris and Warwick boulevards. The War Memorial Museum lies a few blocks south on Warwick. The Living Museum, the only one of its kind east of the Mississippi, presents birds and beasts in natural settings, combining elements of a terrarium, aquarium, botanical garden, planetarium, and zoo. More than 50 species of birds fly in a two-story aviary. Bald eagles, rehabilitated after being shot by hunters, fix a commanding eye on the visitor. A bobwhite whistles from a bush. Enough animals for an Ark — raccoons, foxes, beavers, bobcats, possums, otters, turtles, bees, starfish — scamper, clamber, swim, and fly close to viewers.

The innovative Peninsula Fine Arts Center — "Where There's Something Always New" — seems to be forever putting up or taking down an exhibition in quarters in the Mariners Museum Park. Beginning with a small staff, it drew on volunteers. Most any time a visitor backstage finds the museum's guild members as well as Junior Leaguers and others on ladders with paint brushes and hammers.

"Because we don't yet have a permanent collection, we stay on the edge of many facets of the arts," said Taylor C. Wells, executive director. "It is as if we are a continuing anthology of what's going on in visual arts."

Don't take for granted the War Memorial Museum. It will ambush you. From the looks of the grounds, bristling with big guns, including an atomic cannon with a barrel as long as a telephone pole, you might conclude that soldiers of fortune have holed up inside. But the museum, which lies in Huntington Park on the James River, is as much about peace as war. True, it houses more than 20,000 artifacts from every war we fought from 1776 to today; but among them are wartime posters promoting recruitment and sales of savings bonds. In a section of black citizens' contributions in wartime is a letter home from a soldier in Italy describing his reactions from having attended a picnic where blacks and whites were on an equal footing.

At left, workers gaze in awe at the great overhanging cliff of the USS Eisenhower's bow. Facing page: Three helmeted shipyard workers enjoy a moment of relaxation at the sub's launching.

A memorial to the workers, tugboat Dorothy, the shipyard's first hull, finds a snug harbor in front of the main offices, left. Collis P. Huntington, above, founder of the shipyard and the city, pauses with his nephew, Henry, and a newsboy.

Bald eagles, though handicapped from injuries, retain their regal stare, right. An aviary permits free flight of birds in the Living Museum, below.

An atomic cannon, its snout lifted, dominates the entrance to the War Memorial Museum, right.

At left, a shipwright demonstrates carving to a family visiting the Mariners Museum. Below, eager children practice crafts in the Peninsula Art Center.

PENINSULA ART CENTER

At left, a gigantic eagle figurehead spreads golden wings in the foyer of the Mariners Museum.

MARINERS MUSEUM (2)

55

After World War I when naval appropriations dried up, Homer L. Ferguson of Newport News shipyard persuaded Archer Huntington, the son of founder Collis, to fund a museum devoted to the seas and those who sail them. He also envisioned a 550-acre park fronting the James River. So the Mariners Museum came into being. Landscaping the park kept 200 men busy. Archer's wife, Anna, a tiny, dynamic artist, peopled the park with mammoth granite statuary.

In the Mariners Museum, the visitor is greeted by a gleaming 1½-ton golden eagle with a wingspread of 18½ feet, a figurehead from the U.S. Navy frigate Lancaster. At the other end of the scale from the eagle are 16 exquisite miniatures of ships crafted by August F. Crabtree. As a youth he worked on ships in Vancouver but his heart was with the miniatures. Another galllery is devoted to marine architect William Gibbs, who designed the liner United States. In the carving gallery, a woodcarver works among 20 lifelike figureheads, including one of singer Jenny Lind, that once accented the bows of tall sailing ships. A separate building harbors an international collection of small crafts from primitive skin boats to a Venetian gondola. And looking around, the visitor notices that the museum is filled with spectators of all ages. Many of them — small boys, teenagers, youths in uniform, and old men from the sea — don't ordinarily frequent museums. But then the sea is a democratic institution.

The city was planned from birth by "the father of Newport News," Collis P. Huntington, who began his career at 13 as an apprentice of a Connecticut farmer. From a monthly wage of $7, he saved $84 and earned his release. He peddled wares six years along the East Coast. At 21, he entered a general merchandise business with an older brother in Oneonta, N.Y., and went to California in 1849.

In Sacramento, he and Mark Hopkins founded a hardware firm to provision prospectors. Its second floor became headquarters for pushing the Central Pacific Railroad across California's Sierra Nevada. Hopkins kept the books; Leland Stanford, a grocer, became Governor and wielded influence for the railroad; Charles Crocker supervised construction; and Huntington went east to win financing and lobby Congress, "the hungriest set of men ever got together." The Big Four rushed tracks eastward, gobbling up adjoining land, to a junction near Ogden, Utah, with the Union Pacific, which had been racing westward from Omaha. Huntington became dominant in the Central Pacific and soon headed the transcontinental Southern Pacific. In 1869, he acquired the Chesapeake and Ohio Railway and extended it from Huntington, W.Va., to Richmond and thence, in 1880, 74 miles to deep water at the tip of the Virginia Peninsula. The hamlet of a few scatttered farms and 500 souls was known as Newport News (named, most historians agree, for ship captain Christopher Newport, who brought the settlers to Jamestown in 1607).

Through his Old Dominion Land Co., Huntington

bought 17,000 acres and set about building a city, starting with the six-story Warwick Hotel, which housed, for a time, government offices, a newspaper, the county court, and a bank. The land company also nurtured a chapel, schools, houses, and a utilities company. Huntington transmitted energy to anything he touched.

In 1886, he opened a repair yard to serve the ships that came to fetch coal. He succeeded, he said, in his purpose to start a shipyard in the best location in the world: "It is right at the gateway to the sea. There is never any ice in the winter, and it is never so cold but what you can hammer metal out of doors."

A century later it had grown into the largest privately owned shipyard anywhere and, with upwards of 30,000 workers, Virginia's largest private employer. It has built more than 700 military and civilian ships, including most of the Navy's aircraft carriers. It is the only firm that builds the Nimitz-class nuclear carrier and the only one in the United States capable of building and servicing a full range of surface and submersible ships.

An associate described Huntington's "ample form clad in a tightly buttoned black Prince Albert coat, a broad, deep chest, and a head which speaks for itself. In stature he is six feet one and of full weight. He is putting on his black silk skull cap, but you catch the glimpse of a massive cranium, bald all over its upper surface, with a fringe of grizzled hair below. A heavy mustache falls over his mouth like a waterfall and unites with the full white beard in concealment of the strong square jaw. He is a striking figure as he stands there, with his dark, powerful hand on the doorknob — a personality full of force, dignity, and magnetism. . . ."

He lived to work. When somebody asked why he worked so hard, he replied, "I don't work hard, I work easy." His work was his play. He put together railways, steamship lines, dozens of corporations as persons today play Monopoly. Most biographies treat Newport News and the shipyard in a paragraph as mere way stops in his transcontinental career. But photographs of his New York office show him, massive in mandarin cap, at his desk, and, on the wall at his back, a huge picture of his shipyard, "the world's best half acre," as he called it at the start. Orders to his agents disclose a tenderness for the shipyard that did not extend to any of his other properties. He pushed the builders of the Central Pacific to lay track ever faster. "Let the paint and putty boys come later," he exhorted. But he wrote of ships as if they were living things. He abided with fortitude the yard's substantial losses in the early years. He instructed a shipyard executive: "I would rather lose money on a first-class ship than to make money on one that did not give satisfaction to the Government, and what I want is to get a reputation for building first-class ships, and then always build ships to sustain that reputation. I find

In the dawning day, watermen tong for oysters in the James River, left.

A child investigates the silent, white-sheeted landscape in snow-filled Mariners Museum Park, at right. A guitarist, with a mighty sunset as a backdrop, relaxes in the Mariners Museum Park, below.

MARINERS MUSEUM

SCOTT KINGSLEY

Houses in Hilton Village, built during World War I, have multiplied in value as highly desirable, right. Facing page: An opening in the leaves discloses a peaceful scene as youngsters fish in the Newport News City Park.

DENNIS TENNANT

there is more money made in doing things this way; and, outside of money, there is a great satisfaction in doing work well, and it would be humiliating to me to have anything turned out from our yard that was not first class."

"First class" ran through his conversation and correspondence on the shipyard. "Of all things," Huntington wrote, "I think ships that sail the seas should have honest work — and only that — in all particulars." Out of such sentiments the shipyard's seventh president, Homer L. Ferguson, fashioned a motto, engraved in bronze on a block of granite in the yard: "We shall build good ships here, at a profit if we can, at a loss if we must, but always good ships."

Ferguson led the shipyard through two world wars. The housing shortage of World War I prompted him to build, with the federal government's aid, Hilton Village, the first government subsidized housing project. It remains, with values multiplied, as one of the city's most desirable neighborhoods. In the lean years between wars, the company bid low to get the job of refitting the liner Leviathan, which had been converted to a troopship. As a throng watched it come up the James River, many wept for joy. It was bread on the water — and the company lost more than a million dollars on the $6 million contract. "It held together the work force," Ferguson noted. During World War II, the shipyard of 50,000 workers produced 8 aircraft carriers, 8 cruisers, 18 landing ships (tank), 11 landing ships (dock), and 243 Liberty Ships. "Among the companies which gave our fleet the power to attack, yours has been preeminent," Navy Secretary James Forrestal wrote Ferguson.

Learning that the shipyard's first hull, the tugboat Dorothy launched in December 1890, was languishing in the Elizabeth River mud, shipyard President John P. Diesel said, "Bring her home!" They did, and volunteers, working from original drawings, restored her "sweet shape" and placed her in front of the shipyard's headquarters. On June 19, 1976, she was dedicated "to the men and women of Newport News Shipbuilding."

Raymond K. Davis, her former captain, remarked, "She has everything that a good hull should have in the way of a shape. She's not straight anywhere, nothing straight about her. She's not a real dry ship; she's a little wet in a wind-sea, but she'll take the heavy swells and ride 'em out good." And she's there now, jaunty as a duck, the pride of the yard.

In the 1980s, the shipyard set financial records year after year and rose to the top among the operating segments of Tenneco Inc. with which it had merged in 1968. President Edward J. Campbell attributed success to improved contracts, reduced costs, advanced technology "and most of all to the ability of the shipbuilders of Newport News to adapt and change with the times."

The shipyard stretches three miles along the James River. It never closes down. Viewed at night from the opposite shore, the golden, burning strand pulses with the energy tapped by Collis P. Huntington.

KENNETH SILVER

Poquoson

HERB BARNES

Dictionaries define a pocosin as a low, flat, swampy region. That describes how the land lies in Poquoson, but doesn't catch the spirit of that city of 10,000 which touches the North Poquoson River, the Back River, and the eastern Chesapeake Bay. Highway signs proclaim PRIDE IN POQUOSON, condemning litter, but they could signify the community's pride in many things, especially its schools as exemplified in its high-stepping high school band. To retain the school, Poquoson gave up part of itself.

In 1932, Poquoson, then a district in York County, floated a bond issue and built the high school which also accepted youths from the rest of the county. In 1950, reports spread that York planned to convert the high school into an elementary school and bus Poquoson's teenagers elsewhere.

"Poquoson's people are independent, determined to get the best they can for their children," said Jessie Forrest, president of the Poquoson Historical Commission. "To keep our high school, the community incorporated into a town in 1952. Farmers at the north end, fearing that taxes would become exorbitant, withdrew into what became the Bethel District of Yorktown."

So the conversion into a town wasn't without sacrifice? "It was worth it to have our school," Mrs. Forrest replied. "My people are not inclined to ask for help if it is at all possible to do for themselves. We were taught that when you accepted a handout, you were obligating yourself to something in return."

Poquoson is a workplace for watermen and a bedroom community for employes at Newport News Shipbuilding, NASA and Langley Air Force Base, Fort Monroe, Fort Eustis, and the Coast Guard and Training Station at Yorktown. "Excellent individuals move here," Mrs. Forrest said. "Persons inclined to work for civic betterment recognize that in each other." When there was a move just across the border in Hampton to clear the site of the home of George Wythe, teacher of John Marshall and Thomas Jefferson, she noticed that men from NASA were doing most of the work. "A man from Massachusetts who lives in Gloucester and works at Langley invited me to watch," she said.

Watermen are holding their own in the community's mix. "Certainly they are more visible now," she said. "It used to be a matter of each man doing his own thing. Now there's a watermen's association. Many young men are going to the water. They get a college degree, come home, give momma the diploma, and buy a boat."

The islanders, as they call themselves, are inclined to

The Poquoson High School Band, widely traveled, plays at home for the annual Seafood Festival.

61

In a feeding frenzy,
bluefish take menhaden
while fishermen take
bluefish, above.

In a placid scene, two
teenage sisters wade
near the piers off
Messick Road, left.
Facing page: A great
egret pauses reflectively
as it prowls mudflats for
prey.

be, at once, self-sufficient and sharing. "When we were children in the Depression, our families may have been poor on paper, but we never realized it. We never lacked warm clothing, shelter, and food. And this has been a sharing place. After men came in from fishing and crabbing and left some of the catch with their families, it was look for the nearest handicapped person or widow.

"In the storm of Aug. 23, 1933, the way the families helped each other was beautiful, and they waded in water above their knees to save the animals. A man didn't have a porch so he put a cow in the kitchen. Another saw a calf drifting by and pulled it in. An old sow with four piglets was told to climb a plank, six inches wide, extending from the ground to a second-floor loft, and she went right up, with her offspring behind her, as if they had been practicing it every day."

City Manager Robert M. Murphy, a veteran of four localities, says he can't imagine a jurisdiction that has more community spirit than does Poquoson. When the high school football team defeated one from Eastern Shore's Arcadia, its first victory in four years, the celebration would have befit a bowl game. When the band, the Islanders, marches down the road, leading the parade for the annual Seafood Festival, pride fairly pulsates with the music. The band, which practices daily and travels widely, is supported by the community's fund-raising projects.

In the Festival parade a float, led by Lillian Rollins, is decorated with pine branches, bayberry, gall bushes, and waterfront gear and graced by older folks in exaggerated country costumes, who call themselves the Marsh Mud Family, a tongue-in-cheek portrayal of early Poquoson as outsiders might have imagined it. The float usually wins first place.

Only Northern Virginia localities have higher household incomes than does Poquoson, Murphy said. The population doubled from the 1960s to the 1980s, and there's room for it to double again. Most residents hope it won't. "I don't think we're for manufacturing or traditional industry," Murphy said, "but we're interested in the Peninsula's continuing economic health."

The city has no downtown. Its first traffic light was installed in 1982 at Wythe Creek Road and Little Florida with two banks and a minimarket. (Years ago residents of a neighborhood boasted they caught more fish, grew better corn, and had fairer weather until finally somebody jeered, "Call it Little Florida.") In Poquoson all roads but one lead to the water, so the bull islanders have ample fishing, sailing, swimming, and eating of seafood. There's debate over the nickname's origin. One explanation is that cows, allowed to graze in the marshes, moved for warmth to higher ground at night so that visitors were startled to find herds walking about and lying in the roads.

"The saying is," Mrs. Forrest said, "a bull islander tends to get very difficult to live with if he's moved out of Poquoson."

South of the James

Smithfield, in Isle of Wight County, is renowned for the ham that bears its name. To bask in the fame of such a ham would suffice for almost any town, but Smithfield, on a bluff overlooking the Pagan River's marshes, shifting colors from sedge brown to spring chartreuse to summer green, is attractive itself. It has 32 homes built before 1850. After the Civil War there was a pause and then a building spree that produced 33 Victorian dwellings. All 65 are mapped for a walking tour on shaded streets.

The Virginia Landmarks Register dubbed them an historic district, "perhaps the best preserved of Virginia's Colonial seaports." The oldest is the 1752 courthouse, now housing the Chamber of Commerce. Smithfield has a Little Theater, a ballet studio, and a well-stocked branch of the regional Walter C. Rawls Library of Courtland. The Isle of Wight Museum, a former bank with a Tiffany-style domed skylight, displays Indian artifacts, Civil War relics, and a reproduction of an old-fashioned country store.

"We know we can't help growing, but we're trying to control it," said Mayor Florine Moore. "We enjoy being small. It makes for a close community. People work together and it takes that to get good things done. Smithfield's old homes that have been lived in and loved offer a sense of continuity so that new owners really care about them."

Town Manager Elsey Harris lives next door to Mayor Moore. When he has official papers for her, he drops them off at her back door.

"It saves postage," she said.

Most of Isle of Wight's growth is in the north near the James River Bridge, where "people like to sleep in the peace and quiet of the rural area and work in the city," said Henry H. Bradby, chairman of the Board of Supervisors. "We're doing all we can to see that the development is of high quality."

In Isle of Wight is sturdy St. Luke's Church, dominated by a huge, squat tower that could, from its looks, serve as a fort in an Indian uprising. The Virginia Landmarks Register calls the survivor of the 17th century "the purest expression of Gothic architecture standing in the United States." For three centuries, the church "formed the New World's most direct link with the architectural glories of the Middle Ages."

In Smithfield, two of Windsor Castle's rust-red barns (the first and the third in line) were built about 1725.

ROBERT HART

In Surry County is Bacon's Castle, sole high-style Jacobean manor house of brick in the United States. It isn't a castle, at least not like those in fairy tales; and rebel Nathaniel Bacon Jr., for whom it is named, probably never was in it, but the facts are colorful enough. Built in 1665 for merchant-planter Arthur Allen, the three-story dwelling is set amid linden trees off a country road. Brick walls are three feet thick at the base. Two slim, square towers, centered in the front and rear of the house and rising more than two stories, form with the main rectangular structure the shape of a cross. Soaring from baroque curvilinear gables at each end of the steeply pitched roof is a cluster of three chimneys set diagonally as diamonds.

The Virginia Landmarks Register calls it "the state's if not the nation's outstanding example of 17th century domestic architecture." Castles usually are a frowning lot, but Bacon's Castle, in faded pink brick amid centuries-old trees at the end of the shaded lane, seems, with its projecting front tower, to be stepping forward, ladylike, to greet the visitor. It withstood quietly the sieges of time and Bacon's rebels.

Folk history depicts Bacon as defying tyrannical Gov. William Berkeley by leading disgruntled planters against marauding Indians. In modern histories Berkeley emerges as upholding the law and Bacon as a mercurial adventurer and persecutor of friendly Indians as well as a rising defender of representative government. In August 1676, 70 of his men seized the Allen house and held it three months. In October, Bacon died of fever in Gloucester. Life seeped out of the rebellion. In December, a merchant ship sailed up the James River to the plantation's shore, and the captain sent an order for surrender of the Castle. The rebels scurried away in the night, pockets and pillowcases stuffed with plunder. Other occupants have been gentler. In December 1838, Dr. Emmett Robinson inscribed on a window pane a love letter to his wife, Indiana Allen Henley, and then in 1840 added a poem to Indy: "In storm or sunshine, joy or strife, / Thou art my own — my much loved wife, / The treasured blessing of my life." Georgia's Sidney Lanier, stationed at nearby Burwell's Bay during the Civil War, visited "the dear old castle" and its owner's brown-eyed daughter, Virginia Hankins.

Tales of friendly ghosts cling to the Castle. Former curator Richard Rennolds wouldn't let ghost hunters wire it. "I felt I had a deal with the ghost," he said, "and if it wouldn't go around shouting 'Boo,' I wouldn't let anybody bother it. I think it was a she." About 3:30 one morning, Rennolds woke to the laughing of his 2½-year-old son in an upstairs bedroom. "Daddy, where's the lady?" he asked, when Rennolds bent over his crib. "What lady?" Rennolds asked

"The lady with the white hands. She was tickling me," the child said.

Serene Bacon's Castle, at right, once fell in the hands of rebel band.

ROBERT HART (2)

In reports of caretaker G.I. Price, the ghost appeared as "Bacon's light." Recounting a sighting for me, he said: "I was standing, waiting in the evening for my wife to shut up the chickens when a light, about the size of a jack-me-lantern, came out of an old loft door and went up a little — well, it had to, to get over those trees — and traveled by, just floating along, 40 feet in the air, toward the old graveyard."

"If Mr. Price said he saw it," Rennolds said, "I will take it to the bank. He was a very honest man."

In 1983, archaeologist Nicholas Luccketti, digging into a 19th century garden, found signs of one in the 18th century. "Keep digging," said the Garden Club of Virginia, financing it. He did, and reached a 72,000-square-foot vegetable and herb garden of 1680, "the largest, earliest, best-preserved, most sophisticated garden that has come to light in North America."

Near Bacon's Castle is Chippokes Plantation State Park, named for a friendly Indian chief of yore. "The nicest thing about Chippokes," Parks Commissioner Ben Bolen once said,. "is that you don't feel there's anything that you HAVE to see. It's a restful park. There's no great outstanding feature about it unless you count the broad beautiful views across the James." The 1,600-acre working plantation, stretching along the river's south bank, has been in use more than 375 years.

From the heights the visitor looks across Chippokes Bay to Jamestown. Down river the white-domed beehives of Virginia Power's nuclear plant peep above the trees. Since Bolen characterized the park in 1972, a swimming pool, a gift shop, biking and walking trails, and a visitors center and museum have been added and work has begun on restoring the frame River House, built in the 1700s. The larger Greek Revival mansion was built in 1854. Heading a public fund drive for the park and looking after its welfare in the Virginia General Assembly is State Sen. Elmon Gray of Waverly.

The mansion, built in 1854, became the home of Mr. and Mrs. Victor Stewart. He wished to leave the plantation to the state and after his death she saw to it. The frail little woman used a walker, and when she needed something, she blew a whistle. Bolen remembered: "If you weren't aware of what she was going to do, the blast from that whistle would just about knock you off your chair."

Generous with others, she was frugal with herself. Once she asked Bolen if he'd send her some memo pads that his office might receive as advertising giveaways. He bought several for her, but she mailed them back. "These are too costly," she wrote. "Take them back to the store and send me cheaper ones."

On the third weekend in July there's a Pork, Pine, and Peanut Festival offering arts and crafts and good things to eat. The landscape — hazy fields and deep forests under the eye of a slowly circling hawk — seems

Old St. Luke's squat tower looks as if it could repel Satan's minions.

unhurried. After viewing the power company's massive reactors, visitors may drop into the park — and into another century — for decompression.

The nuclear plant generates 70 percent of Surry's tax base. Most of the new money has been invested in enriching what had been one of Virginia's poorest school systems. It now ranks third among the state's school districts in the amount spent per pupil. "There are many ills in our communities," said M. Sherlock Holmes, chairman of the Board of Supervisors, "and we feel if we can educate our people, we can solve many of our problems. Even now we don't have as many looking for public assistance. We just feel a better educated person makes a better citizen."

Southampton County leads with 30,000 acres in farming peanuts in Virginia and is No. 1 in the nation. "In hard times," a farmer told me, "we lived on peanuts and past recollections."

The past recollected includes two brilliant generals, and a Virginia Governor. As for peanuts, a patch of counties has the nation's best varieties, soils, and weather conditions, says extension agronomist Allen H. Allison. (The other counties are Sussex, Greensville, Isle of Wight, Surry, Dinwiddie, Prince George. Suffolk gained 16,000 acres of peanuts when it merged with Nansemond in 1974.)

"The plant is a unique legume," Allison said. "Bushes bear yellow aerial flowers that produce shoots, 'pegs,' which grow downward until they penetrate the soil two inches. The peg's tip, containing the ovary, turns horizontally, swells, and grows in darkness into the mature peanut. The process requires 150 days, and," Allison said with enthusiasm, "after studying it many, many years, we still don't know a lot about it."

A machine breaks the ground in March. A mechanical planter begins dropping the seed during May and June. When the plants crack the ground, a weeder or rotary hoe loosens the soil. When the peanuts mature, a digging machine pulls the plants together from two rows and turns them upside down so the peanuts dry in the sun. Three or so days later a combine with a revolving pickup head scoops up the vines, separates the peanuts, throws the vines out back for hay, blows the peanuts into a cage atop the machine and dumps them with a hydraulic lift into drying wagons or bins. Warm air blows through the loads to dry the peanuts.

The farmer hauls them to a buying point where an inspector grades them for sale. Virginia's peanut crop grosses $90 million. One man and a machine do work that used to require a dozen families and 18 mules. "Every mule in Southampton County is too old to vote," a farmer said. "You can't even buy a mule collar in this county today."

Century-old Isle of Wight Courthouse retains a quiet dignity, top. In Smithfield, the Old Isle of Wight Courthouse houses the Chamber of Commerce, bottom.

JIM PILE (2)

ROBERT HART

Southampton's other major crop is fine paper. In hard times after the Civil War, the Camp family of six brothers and two sisters infused the town of Franklin and surrounding counties with energy, a growing payroll, and liberal gifts. Three brothers went to Florida, but Paul D. Camp, or "Pay Day" as he was called, and his younger brothers, Robert J. and James L. Camp, engaged in lumbering and bought in 1877 a steam sawmill across the Blackwater River in Isle of Wight County and formed in 1888 the Camp Manufacturing Co. In 1936, in partnership with the Chesapeake Corporation of Virginia, the firm began producing pulp and paper in a mill next to the sawmill. In 1945, the association with Chesapeake Corporation was dissolved. The second generation, Hugh and James L. Camp Jr., merged with Union Bag and Paper Co. in 1956 to form what became Union Camp Corp. Two decades of expansion ensued, and 1968 marked the start of $57 million in construction. The Franklin complex, with the largest paper printing mill in the world, is headquarters for Union Camp's fine paper division. Nearly 2,600 employes earn more than $70 million a year.

The Camps' biographer, Parke Rouse, said, "They are wonderful people," close as a family, powerful, extremely generous, and marvelous to their help and the community. There are five foundations, one by Union Camp and four by members of the family. They make annual gifts to public service projects throughout the state, especially in southern Virginia. Franklin has a YMCA, thanks to them, that any city would envy."

On Feb. 22, 1973, the Union Camp Corp. deeded 49,000 acres in Virginia's Dismal Swamp to The Nature Conservancy for a wildlife refuge. Weyerhaeuser Co. donated 12,000 acres. The Interior Department bought land to round out the refuge to 120,000 acres. Corporate farms and subdivisions had been nibbling at the swamp. Without Union Camp's rescue, it would have been lost.

In 1985, Union Camp Corp. donated to Old Dominion University 320 acres of the Zuni Pine Barrens along the Blackwater River. The Blackwater Ecologic Preserve contains the northernmost population of longleaf pines, the plant, ODU biologist Lytton J. Musselman observed, that "helped build Norfolk" in providing masts, turpentine, and pitch for ships. Hogs devoured the young pines' terminal buds, nearly extirpating it in Virginia. A decrease in the frequency of fires, as settlers turned woods into cropland, also endangered the pine. Fire, the longleaf's friend, removes competing growth. The seedling's delicate growing point escapes by lying low, beneath the fire line. When, during puberty, the pine shoots up several feet a year, it develops fireproof bark.

The barrens contain species found nowhere else in

A turn of the road in Isle of Wight presents such enticing sights as Wrenn's Mill and water rushing over stones, left.

69

At right, nuclear power station in Surry enriches tax base — and schools. Below, Nelle Pitman and her daughter Helen explore the candy jar in the country store gallery of the Isle of Wight Museum.

An ecologic preserve, given by Union Camp Corp., is a rhapsody in green on the Blackwater River, right. Facing page: Pink lightning stabs dark skies above an Isle of Wight cornfield.

Virginia. The Zuni area is "an island of plants, disjunct" from populations farther south. Traveling a few miles, "you're journeying, in effect, hundreds of miles south to a community of plant life that was once characteristic of much of this region."

The region has had rare individuals including George Henry Thomas, a person of moral and physical stamina who fought with the North in the Civil War. Historians rate him among its three top generals. He had to overcome suspicions about his Southern origins. "Let the Virginian wait," Abraham Lincoln advised. Thomas saved the Army of the Cumberland at Chickamauga when his corps' battle line bent into a horseshoe shape but did not break, enabling Gen. William Rosecrans' army to retreat. At Nashville, ignoring Gen. Ulysses S. Grant's impatience, he waited until his troops were ready and then smashed Gen. John Bell Hood's Rebel army. His men called him "Pap" and "Slow-Foot." In an age when other generals ordered massed troops to rush modern artillery, he thought first of his men.

Legends still circulate about Thomas, who never returned to Southampton. His three sisters turned his picture to the wall. Shortly after the war, the federal commander in Petersburg took a wagon of provisions to Thomaston, but the sisters refused it. "We have no brother," the oldest, Judith, told him. He died, she said, on April 17, 1861, the day Virginia seceded. A happier legend suggests that because of his influence Southampton never suffered invasion.

In July 1985, the county's historical society met at Thomaston under an oak where he had played as a child. They unveiled a marker honoring him as being "loyal to conscience, country and family." The metal marker's other side salutes Alma Ruth Davis, a ballerina who retired from New York after a bout with tuberculosis. She restored Thomaston, undertook organic farming, and preached about the perils of pesticides. She and her two sisters decided to leave Thomaston "to someone who had loved it," Lisa Drake, a college student who lived across the road and had become to Davis the daughter she never had.

Southampton was also the home of Maj. Gen. William Mahone, Confederate hero at Petersburg's Battle of the Crater. After the war he consolidated three railroads into what became the Norfolk & Western Railway. He led the Readjuster Movement aimed at scaling down the state debt. When he went to the U.S. Senate, he lined up in 1881 with the national Republicans and won control of Virginia's black vote — moves that cost him white votes when he ran unsuccessfully for governor in 1889. He shook Virginia's politics to its roots.

In the courthouse at Courtland is a portrait of Colgate W. Darden Jr. in a white summer suit, seated at his desk, books within reach, his hand to his chin. The canvas catches Darden after he had been Congressman, Governor, president of the University of Virginia. Ahead were eight years on the State Board of Education

where he worked with Lewis F. Powell Jr. to upgrade schools. Darden's nearly lifelong concern culminated in a mandate in the Virginia Constitution that every child have a chance at a quality education.

Both Darden and Powell had family roots in Southampton, and Powell was born in Suffolk. After Powell's teamwork with Darden, his next public service was as a justice on the U.S. Supreme Court. On a bench divided between moderates and conservatives, Justice Powell, following the law, the Constitution, and his conscience, became the man in the middle, the majority maker. The tall, slim, courtly figure, quiet-spoken and courteous, epitomizes the best in the Virginia tradition.

Darden, who was always "projecting" on works for the public good, gave Hampton Roads' Boy Scouts a camp near his boyhood home in Southampton. When they outgrew it, he rebought it for $25,000 to help them buy a larger site in Surry County. Then he gave the former Boy Scout Camp to the Girl Scouts. Lions and Kiwanis clubs began raising money to equip the new camp. Darden gave $6,000 for roads and then visited 50 clubs urging them to "invest in youth," matching whatever they gave. One night as he and Tim Timmons were driving to Darden's home in Norfolk after a meeting, Darden sighed and said, "Well, I guess I've just euchered myself out of another $1,000."

As the car traveled ruts in Darden's drive, Timmons asked, "Colgate, why in hell don't you have this driveway repaired?"

"Tim," he replied, "I just can't scratch up the money to do it."

Darden believed in solving problems through calm reason and humor. What he said, expressing himself freely and thereby stimulating debate, was as important as what he did.

He was among those seeking to ease the stress of desegregating schools although, he once recalled, he had not expected to see it achieved in Southside Virginia in his lifetime. "That prediction just shows what can happen when a chump takes off from the launching pad and begins freewheeling," he said. "It was brought home to me when I attended in Southampton County a celebration for the winning football team. The gymnasium was packed with blacks and whites, and they showed no difference in their enthusiasm for the team. And that celebration took place on the very ground where Nat Turner's insurrection, the largest slave revolt in the United States, had occurred."

At night in the courthouse's glassed-walled foyer, Darden's portrait is lit. From the road, the seated figure, his hand to his chin as he ponders, has a three-dimensional effect, as if he is there, projecting.

In savory surroundings, S. Wallace Edwards Jr. and Samuel W. Edwards III, father and son, stand amid hams in their firm's aging room, right. Facing page: Every spring a shad planking occurs near Wakefield, when the shad (and the politicians) begin to run.

BOB BROWN

MICHELE McDONALD

Suffolk

When the City of Suffolk merged with Nansemond on Jan. 1, 1974, it grew overnight from a population of 9,985 to 45,024 and from 2 square miles to 430, half the size of Rhode Island. Until the merger, Suffolk hungered for land, and Nansemond County, which surrounded Suffolk, coveted city services. In 1972, seeking to fend off an annexation suit by Suffolk, as well as one from Portsmouth, Nansemond County temporarily had become a city, but an annexation court suggested that Suffolk and Nansemond unite, which they did, with the approval of voters in each city.

On Jan. 3, Nansemond Mayor D.J. Mangum Jr. presented a 2.5-foot key of his city to James F. Hope, the Mayor of old Suffolk, and an hour later the Council of the newly merged city elected Hope the Mayor and Mangum the Vice Mayor. In a ceremony outside the Suffolk Municipal Center, Gov. Mills E. Godwin Jr., a Nansemond native, urged a broadening of the new city's economic base to provide jobs and thereby assure greater tax revenues for education. "Few places in Virginia are more richly endowed than this new city," Godwin said. "Few possess any greater potential for the future. We must coordinate our efforts, heal any differences, and think positively about our future and the tools with which we have to work."

Ten years later Suffolk launched a national campaign to attract industry, with Godwin as honorary chairman. Meanwhile, it continued its role as the world's largest manufacturer of peanut products. It and Southampton, the nation's leading producer, are joined in their economies as snugly as two peanuts in a shell.

By the time peanuts are consumed in a candy bar or out of a paper bag at a ballpark or from a plastic packet aboard an airplane, or spread on bread, or put to 500 other uses, the return to Virginia's economy is $225 million annually. The peanut, agronomist Allen H. Allison insists, is the paragon among crops: "It is 26 percent protein, a count higher than that of dairy products and many meats, and it has no cholesterol. Up to 40 per cent of Virginia's crop is exported, helping to offset the country's trade deficit. The peanut doesn't pile up unmanageable surpluses."

In the Holland community of Suffolk, Virginia Tech's 200-acre Tidewater Agricultural Experiment Station works with a staff of 50 to enhance the peanut's shelf life and flavor.

In 1986, the General Assembly appropriated $770,000 for the Station, which also works with other crops. The Station's director, Glen L. Neuberger, ob-

Amid fields of green and gold in Driver, workers harvest the spring crop of kale.

served that its programs are designed to serve Eastern Virginia, which raises 80 percent of the state's soybeans and corn and 60 percent of the swine, as well as most of the peanuts. Frequent droughts in the past decade have moved the Station to investigate methods of irrigation.

The peanut's story is as fraught with irony as are those of tobacco and cotton. European explorers took it from South America to Spain. It spread to Africa as "goobers" (ground nuts) or "pindas," and came to Virginia as the food supply for blacks in slave ships. They planted them around their cabins. In 1844, Dr. Matthew Harris harvested the first commercial crop on his farm in Sussex County on U.S. Route 460, and he walked Petersburg's streets urging people to try peanuts. During the Civil War, Confederates sang about "lying in the shadow underneath the trees, goodness, how delicious, eating goober peas!" Northern soldiers nibbled on peanuts and spread the postwar demand for them. Circus wagons carried them through America. Missionaries took them to China and India.

Suffolk started becoming "the peanut capital of the world" with the arrival of Amedeo Obici from Pennsylvania. In 1888, at 12, he came from Oderza in Italy and worked at his uncle's fruit stand in Scranton. One day, a man shelling and eating peanuts passed the stand. The boy followed and picked up a shell. The stranger gave him the remaining peanuts in the sack — and they gave Amedeo an idea. He bought a sheet of metal from a junkyard and fashioned a roaster. At night he bagged peanuts that he sold by day. After sales peaked at the stand, he put a pair of wagon wheels on the roaster and hawked them through town. When a truck with 100 burlap bags of peanuts pulled up at the fruit stand, his uncle said, "Amedeo, it's time for you to go on your own." In Wilkes-Barre he rented a store and, with slowly accumulating savings, brought his mother, brother, and sisters from Italy. He and brother-in-law Mario Peruzzi rented a factory at $25 a month and hired six persons.

To learn more about the peanut, he visited Suffolk — and stayed. In 1913, he borrowed $25,000 to buy a small brick factory. Plunging into civic activities, he became president of the Rotary Club, exalted ruler of the Elks, chairman of the Chamber of Commerce. Ted J. Lo Cascio, who wrote the "Obici Story," remembers a stocky figure, 5 feet tall, with an imposing air, a large nose, and animated talk. "He was always in motion," said Lo Cascio. Pondering with Peruzzi a name for the enterprise, Amedeo mused, "Planters raise peanuts. Why don't we call it Planters Peanuts?" He offered a $5 award for the best sketch of a symbol. Suffolk schoolboy Anthony Gentile won with a drawing of a peanut in human guise. An artist added cane, spats, top monocle to jaunty Mr. Peanut.

In 1916, Amedeo married Louise Musante, operator of a fruit stand in Wilkes-Barre. Tall, stately, reserved, she was interested in gardening and the arts. The couple took pride in showing the gardens around their

Lone Star Lakes, left behind in marl quarries, afford fishing and room to ruminate, below.

In the evening on Lake Prince, a fisherman casts from his boat in a scene turned taupe by the sun, left. Morning mists veil boats awaiting a day's work on Chuckatuck Creek, above.

home, Bay Point Farm on 350 acres overlooking the Nansemond River. They loved to entertain. One evening, seeing that his guests hesitated to open small bottles of wine at their places for fear of spilling wine on the linen, expansive Obici arose, and, holding his thumb loosely over the mouth of the bottle, shook drops over the table cloth.

His wife dreamed of a hospital for Suffolk. After her death in 1936, he provided funds for building Louise Obici Memorial Hospital and a nursing school and a $20 million endowment to run it. He died in 1947, two years before the hospital was completed. In 1986, another of his foundations supplied $12 million for expanding the hospital. Portsmouth bought the Obici Mansion and built a golf course, which hosts a tournament for the Ladies Professional Golf Association. Some 500 yards away from the mansion is the Planters Club, also built by Obici, purchased by Suffolk for social events.

"With Planters manufacturing peanut products, other facilities developed to shell, clean, and grade peanuts," Allison said. "Allied industries for manufacturing production equipment also settled in Suffolk." Among the shelling plants are Birdsong Peanuts, Gold Kist, Pond Bros. Peanut Co., Parker Peanut Co., and, in Courtland, Hancock Peanut Co. and Virginia-Carolina Peanut Co-op. Hobbs-Adams Co. does worldwide business in building shelling plants and manufacturing farm equipment.

Starting in 1960, Planters went through three mergers to become in 1984 the Planters and Life Savers Division of RJR/Nabisco, with 36 buildings and 38 acres in Suffolk and plants in Chattanooga and Fort Smith, Ark. Planters continues to evince, through sizable gifts, Obici's concern for Suffolk. In 1975, it started, with the help of local and state funds, a program teaching reading and writing and offering the equivalent of a high school diploma. Planters Employe Training, aimed at eliminating illiteracy, became a model for firms throughout North America.

Each October the city hosts a week-long Peanut Fest, featuring a parade, along with shows (art, horse, fashion, crafts), concerts (rock, country), shrimp feast, and a competition for sculpture molded from peanut butter, one usage not even George Washington Carver had envisioned. A visitor can wander about, taking it all in, along with handfuls of peanuts from burlap bags scattered about the route.

Suffolk's cultural centerpiece on North Main Street is Riddick's Folly, built in 1837, and so nicknamed because contemporaries of Mills Riddick, the owner, deemed him presumptuous to want a 21-room, 4-story house. But his wife, Mary Taylor Riddick, bore 14 children. And in that era of the "extended family" when uncles, aunts, and grandparents and occasional cousins lived under one roof, not forgetting guests who settled in for weeks, even the occupants of Riddick's capacious home may have felt crowded now and then.

Riddick, a lumberman who farmed the Dismal

Swamp's cypresses, died in 1844, but the house stayed in the family 130 years, until 1967. In the Civil War, federal troops occupied Suffolk 18 months, and Gen. John J. Peck made the house his headquarters. When a large bed of his choosing wouldn't fit in a smaller upstairs room, he had its four posts sawed short. "General Peck's bed" is still in the family. Another upstairs bedroom became a hospital. Its walls bear the signatures of Union soldiers.

For a decade the mansion served as Nansemond County's school board office, but in 1978, after the merger with Suffolk, a nonprofit group persuaded the city to set aside the mansion as a cultural arts center and museum. In 1986, a fund-raising drive received a boost when the Garland Gray Foundation of Waverly, four Camp foundations, Nabisco Brands and an individual in Franklin issued challenge grants totaling $125,000, half the goal. Nearly a half million dollars was devoted to renovating the mansion's interior.

The center provides period rooms, a library for local historical society, gallery space, meeting rooms for civic groups, two parlors of the 1837 period for social functions, a room for children's activities, and, in the English basement, a gift shop and exhibits on the peanut. All in all, Riddick's Folly has proved a wise investment, sheltering his family more than a century and now serving the large community family of Suffolk.

Farms for breeding, riding, and training horses abound in Hampton Roads. In Suffolk, Jeri Lou Paul has trained champions, including the great Quartermaster, which won two gold medals in the Pan American games in 1987. In 1980, when she was 16, and again in 1982, riding Navigator, she won the junior world championship in working hunters. On the farm Port-o-Call, a family operation, she said, "I'm the rider and stall-mucker wrapped in one."

In 1975, Norfolk's former city manager, G. Robert House Jr., brought his expertise to Suffolk. During six formative years, he looked first to the basic services for the huge city. In 1976, it bought 1,172 acres with 11 lakes that were created during marl-mining begun in the 1920s by the Lone Star Mining Co. An aquifer and springs filled the mined hollows. The city provided first-rate recreational facilities at the Lone Star Lakes Park, and it had the sense to leave untouched most of the wilderness. To assure Suffolk a water supply, House and his assistant and successor, John L. Rowe Jr., obtained 18 federal grants to fund nearly 90 per cent of a $16.8 million water treatment plant installed at the Lone Star Lakes. Shortly after House died in a plane crash in 1982, while city manager of Portsmouth, the Suffolk City Council named the treatment plant for him, a fitting tribute to "a water pioneer" in South Hampton Roads, said then-Mayor George H. Barnett.

A red barn, so bright it seems to generate its own light, blesses U.S. Route 58 near Holland and all who pass that way.

In a poll early in Rowe's tenure, a vast majority said they wouldn't want to live anywhere but Suffolk. They regarded it as a "safe place" to live and raise children and yet they were only a half hour or so from more populous cities of Hampton Roads. Occasionally individuals in their 40s remark that when they enter Suffolk, with its crossroads stores, broad fields, and slow-flowing streams, they feel as if they have stepped back into the 1950s. In the poll, some wished, rather wistfully, that people in neighboring cities realized "how nice Suffolk is." At times they used to feel left out of the family circle. City Manager Rowe, the City Council and Andrew Damiani, then the mayor, decided to publicize Suffolk's amenities. In 1983, 25 formed Suffolk Adventure and worked with the city in raising more than $500,000 for a three-year national advertising campaign. They noted industries that had chosen Suffolk, such as Tetley Tea, Allied Colloids, and 20 businesses related to forestry. They cited the city's Foreign Trade Zone and a commercial park near the Suffolk Municipal Airport with its 5,000-foot runway. Built by the Navy in 1940 about three miles south of downtown, it was purchased by Suffolk for corporate and private planes and improved by federal and state aid of more than $1 million in the mid-1980s.

"We see ourselves as the gateway to Hampton Roads for travelers approaching from the west as well as from the south," Rowe said. "Most modes of transportation come through Suffolk via Routes 58 and 460 and I-664."

From Newport News, I-664 crosses Hampton Roads and ties into northern Suffolk where more than 3,000 acres are zoned for development. In the late 1980s, three developers had purchased land for major projects, one of which, a billion-dollar outlay, would have 7,500 homes. "A city within a city," Rowe characterized it. "To think of the sites that are available in Suffolk near arterial highways and railroads almost boggles the mind. We are hearing from firms looking to establish major distribution centers, much as Golden State Food Supply that settled here in 1985."

One result of an enlarging tax base, Mayor Johnnie Mizelle observed, has been better schools. A $30 million bond issue will fund construction of two new high schools in a five-year program. Raising teachers' salaries put Suffolk on a par with neighboring cities — all of which is reflected in rising test scores for the city's pupils.

Some people wish to keep Suffolk as it was 25 years ago, remarked a veteran legislator, Del. J. Samuel Glasscock, and that's impossible, but to retain the best of it will take planning and follow through to make it work. "We have tremendous opportunities, but it's going to take some doing." he said.

Meanwhile, at the agricultural experiment station, agronomist Allison received a call from a graduate student working for NASA regarding attempts to grow peanuts in space.

ROBIE RAY

Kathy Whitworth strides to victory in Suffolk's LPGA tournament at Portsmouth-owned Sleepy Hole golf course, above. Jeri Lou Paul, champion trainer of hunters and jumpers, guides Caruso over the jump in the training ring, at right. Facing page: Opening day of Bennett's Creek Little League at Driver Field catches the timeless quality of the national pastime.

ERIC THINGSTAD (2)

Portsmouth

Two things are easily remembered about Portsmouth: (1) The natives pronounce it Porchmuth, as if a verandah ran around the city, and (2) it produces more outstanding individuals per capita than any other city in the United States.

Porchmuth prevails, ultimately, even among those who were not born there (just as Isle of Wight becomes Isle of White in the mouths of recent arrivals). Perhaps the aberrant pronunciation rules because there is greater relish in enunciating full-bodied Porchmuth, as if one had a mouthful of hot buttered biscuit, than in saying, precisely, Portsmouth.

The abundance of outstanding persons discloses itself gradually. Often, scanning The New York Times obituaries of famous persons — scientists, actors, doctors — one reads in the last paragraph that the subject was born in Portsmouth, Va. When I mentioned this once to then Virginian-Pilot Editor Robert Mason, he said, "Everybody comes from Portsmouth."

And their names are as prominent in state affairs as in national circles. In a span so brief that their careers overlapped, Portsmouth supplied a Virginia Chief Justice (Lawrence W. I'Anson), a United States Senator (William B. Spong Jr.), a Lieutenant Governor (Richard J. Davis), a Federal District Judge (John A. MacKenzie), and a Congressman (Rep. Porter Hardy Jr.)

To salute the achievements of the notables, a committee winnowed a list of 300 nominees to 100 and then to two dozen and invited them to a banquet in October 1987. Other events that week celebrated the start of a revival of downtown Portsmouth in the 1980s.

Some of the notables didn't recognize their city's downtown, which had undergone a face lift and a renovation of the waterfront that helped fuel the economy. When the City Council hired George L. Hanbury as City Manager, he encouraged projects to lure business. Portsmouth created one of Virginia's first enterprise zones and spent $10 million in improving streets, helping owners install new facades on stores, and creating the new waterfront park — programs totaling $10 million. Developers invested $57 million.

In 1983, there was an increase in Portsmouth's taxable investment, a cause for rejoicing in a city where federal and state agencies take much of the land off the tax rolls. Then investments for 1984 and 1985 were the strongest in the city's history, and the record for 1986 nearly doubled their showings. "If the downtown is deteriorating, the entire municipality does," Hanbury said. "To increase the vitality of the city and really do

The aircraft carrier America moves along after being overhauled at the Norfolk Naval Shipyard.

At right, workers at the Norfolk Naval Shipyard cast replicas of cannon for the USS Constitution. Below, a Coast Guard cutter docks at twilight.

JOHN H. SHEALLY II

DENNIS MOOK (2)

Led by retired Rear Adm. Allen Roby on the Constitution's birthday, citizens dedicate a flag to fly over the harbor on an 80-foot pole, right. Facing page: Cherry-red Portsmouth Lightship is now a museum of Coast Guard history.

MIKE WILLIAMS

almost open heart surgery, drastic improvements had to be undertaken downtown. I'm delighted with the response. It's exceeded my optimistic dreams."

The business community, led by Clyde R. Hoey II, united in the Portsmouth Partnership and raised $1.5 million for the ventures and then set about raising $1 million in 1987.

When Norfolk's Waterside opened, Portsmouth needed something to complement it, "the other side of Waterside." On its own refurbished waterfront, it offered Portside, a fetching pavilion of latticework under a blue and white tent and a glass-walled visitors center. And then the city moved to revive the Portsmouth-Norfolk ferry, which had died in 1955 after the opening of the first of three tunnels between the two cities.

Norfolk and Portsmouth are amphibians, anyway, and they should never have strayed far from the water. Two ferries proved so popular with steadily rising ridership that near the close of 1987, when the customers reached nearly 1 million, Portsmouth began considering launching a third ferry in the Elizabeth River. Not only was it a convenience to persons working in one city and living in the other, but the ferry was fun, an answer to the thrill rides in theme parks, only the ferry was soothing and subtle and cost only 50 cents a trip.

There's always a breeze riffling the broad blue plain of the river. The ferry sloshes along, a cooling sound in itself. Sitting on the top deck, lounging on a worn wooden bench, basking in the sun, you can watch the river traffic — pleasure boats spraying past, a little blue tug pushing four barges, an intelligent sheltie herding sheep — or marvel at the two cities' profiles.

They are siblings, and they work best when they work together. Once, in the Portsmouth Chamber of Commerce's briefing room, I was startled, gazing out a wall-sized third-floor window, to see a strange skyline. After a few seconds it became clear that a section of Norfolk's skyline, thrusting forward from the other side of the river as if on a stereopticon slide, had filled a gap in the Portsmouth mural, commingling, creating a sudden new scene. That's how close the sisters are.

Many a Norfolkian has taken guests to ride on the ferry. When they step off the boat, they experience a sense of adventure almost as if they are in a foreign land, so the natural thing to do is look around, get on a trolley-mobile that conveys them to Olde Towne, winding through streets lined with the largest collection of antique dwellings between Alexandria and Charleston.

A story clings to nearly every dwelling. During the Civil War, the Union general supervising the occupation, Benjamin F. "Beast" Butler, was inspecting the William Peters house, and, when a young woman tripped him on the stairs, silver spoons cascaded out of his uniform. He ran for president with the Greenback Party in 1884. Someone strung a banner — "Butler Hero of Five Forks" — in Portsmouth, and someone else added "and the Lord only knows how many silver teaspoons."

Portsmouth is neighborly. When a citizen, while out of town, is asked where he's from, he, without mentioning the city, says Cradock . . . Truxton . . . Port Norfolk, all of which are historic districts and should not be missed. Portsmouth is patriotic. There are parades and ceremonies at the 1846 Courthouse on the Fourth of July and Memorial Day. Observing the Constitution's Bicentennial, the throng was awaiting the firing of the 9 o'clock gun at the Naval Shipyard, which, for one of the few times in history, was to be allowed to fire at 4 o'clock to start the fun. Some 50 seconds before the hour, a balloon popped, and the crowd began cheering and ringing bells, the first time anybody ever jumped the 9 o'clock gun.

The 1846 Courthouse has a children's museum in the basement and art throughout the upper floors. When relics from the Mary Rose, King Henry VIII's flagship, toured a choice few museums in America, the Courthouse was among them. Nearby is a quaint building, the former Norfolk County Clerk's office, now housing the Virginia Sports Hall of Fame, an institution inspired by articles from Portsmouth sportswriter Abe Goldblatt. It houses memorabilia of outstanding athletes. On the waterfront is the Coast Guard Lightship Museum, a 101-foot cherry-red lightship that served nearly half a century and now is a haven for items of Coast Guard history. A sign of downtown's resurgence was the reopening of the art deco Commodore moviehouse, transformed with a dining area downstairs and the gallery for serious moviegoers. Across High Street another movie theater, the Colony, combined a restaurant with films and combos.

Portsmouth's most storied institution is the Norfolk Naval Shipyard, the name being a longstanding source of regret among many in the city, but a move to change it to Portsmouth always runs into the fact that it would then be confused with the Portsmouth, N.H., shipyard (which is in reality in Kittery, Maine.)

A Scot, Andrew Spruill, established the yard in 1767. By 1775, it had become the "most considerable" yard on the East Coast. It survived being burned by the British in 1779, the U.S. Navy in 1861, and the Confederate Navy in 1862. Its workers are proud that it is the oldest, biggest, and best among the Navy's eight yards. The first two distinctions are incontestable. The third is supported by a stream of honors, including awards for excellence from the Navy, the Senate, and the president.

The Norfolk Naval Shipyard built Drydock Number One, the first in the nation, of large blocks of Massachusetts granite in stepped tiers. It looks to be an exceedingly steep amphitheater quarried out of the ground, a place for a giant to lie down. It is still in use.

The yard's employes do repairs aboard ships, often on the other side of the globe. Some were aboard those invading Grenada. Others were at Beirut during hostilities there. On an average day, the shipyard's workers are aboard 55 ships. Within the yard, 12,300 employes work in seven dry docks and 800 buildings on 1,344

Above, the annual Fourth of July celebration includes a parade that winds through downtown Portsmouth. At left, sailors, dignitaries, townspeople gather on the steps of the 1846 Courthouse to hear Fourth of July oratory.

DENNIS MOOK (2)

Antique houses age gracefully in Portsmouth's Olde Towne, left. Below, Olde Towne abounds in flower boxes and gardens and errant roses.

At left, an old-style street light at twilight marks one of the 20 blocks in Olde Towne.

A young, would-be artist, highly pleased, takes a turn at a communal canvas, right. A fountain on Portsmouth's waterfront becomes a focal point for crowds during the Seawall Art Festival, below.

At right, the Elizabeth River Ferry and the Carrie B enliven Portside. Far right: A yellow umbrella is a bright beacon for an artist displaying work at the Seawall Art Festival.

acres. Their work grosses $750 million a year. Land and facilities are worth over $2 billion.

The Norfolk Naval Shipyard built the first battleship commissioned by the Navy (USS Texas) and the first all-steel ship built completely in a government yard (USS Raleigh). Twice the shipyard shaped history. It converted a burned and sunken steam frigate (USS Merrimack) into an ironclad (CSS Virginia). The Virginia's battle with the USS Monitor in March 1862 doomed wooden warships and introduced steel ships to the world's navies.

After Billy Mitchell's bombers demonstrated air power by sinking a captured German battleship in Chesapeake Bay, the Navy ordered in 1921 the building of a ship capable of launching airplanes. Norfolk Naval Shipyard converted the collier USS Jupiter into a flattop with a flight deck 520 feet long and 65 feet wide. It was named the USS Langley for aviation pioneer Samuel Pierpont Langley. It had no superstructure, so the bridge was below the deck. When the phone lines failed, runners rushed messages between the flight deck and the bridge below it. The Langley proved itself, and the Saratoga, the Lexington, and the Ranger followed in time to help turn the tide in the Pacific during World War II. (The Langley was sunk in the Battle of the Java Sea in 1943.)

No longer a shipbuilder, the Norfolk Naval Shipyard is the world's largest yard for repairing, overhauling, and modernizing warships. When an aircraft carrier, having been overhauled, moves down the Southern Branch of the Elizabeth River on its way back to the Norfolk Naval Base, its superstructure looms as large as the tallest building on the banks, and the river, nearly filled with the big ship, suddenly seems to have shrunk to the size of a creek. Looking up one day from work in his Portsmouth office, newspaperman Ron Speer watched a carrier moving by — and realized the $3 billion vessel was worth far more than all the property, valued at $1.9 billion, in the city it was passing.

"The strength of the shipyard is not docks, buildings, 2.8 million hand tools, 400 cranes, and hundreds of major industrial machines," says Joe M. Law, its public affairs officer. "That distinction belongs to the men and women who come from dozens of cities and villages of Virginia and North Carolina. They earn $340 million a year while forming an award-winning team whose members often think of it as 'family.' Indeed the shipyard is a major force in many family traditions, with one clan known to have worked continuously in the yard since 1830."

In 1986, a request came from Boston asking the shipyard to cast two eight-foot long cannon for the USS Constitution, "Old Ironsides." The yard responded as volunteers made the molds, poured the molten metal, and cast the only authentic cannon among the 16 on the ship. "It seemed appropriate that, for the nation's oldest ship, the nation's oldest shipyard should do the work," said Cmdr. Joseph Z. Brown.

Chesapeake

In the early 1960s, state assemblymen sometimes accused Chesapeake of counting bears in its census for representation, but by the mid-1980s it had become the state's second fastest growing city (behind Virginia Beach) with a population of 140,226 and a projected 200,000 by the year 2000. With 353 square miles, it is the state's second largest city (after Suffolk), thanks to the merger in 1963 of Norfolk County and the City of South Norfolk.

Noting that a comprehensive land use plan is in the offing, Mayor Sidney M. Oman said, "I see Chesapeake as the biggest country-city in the U.S.A." Residents cherish the rural heritage. Newspaperman Bob Geske, trying to decide among job offers, chose the one in Chesapeake. "It was the only city I could see in the United States where you could buy a license to hunt bear," he said. "You don't get many chances like that."

The bears have a permanent place in Chesapeake's population. In the Great Dismal Swamp National Wildlife Refuge, which Chesapeake shares with Suffolk and North Carolina, black bears move about without regard to boundary lines, Hampton Roads' first denizens to recognize the commonality of its parts. When sighted on a trail, they fade phantom-like into the brush.

Human inhabitants are highly visible and vocal. "The individual citizen still feels that he or she can speak and be heard on issues of local government," said City Manager James W. Rein. The City Council's meetings are among Virginia's liveliest as its members struggle valiantly to reconcile their constituents' desire for new industry with their longing for a bucolic environment. In a spring meeting in 1987, a shop owner wished to locate in a residential neighborhood "because of its peaceful atmosphere," but 30 residents asserted that the shop would disturb the peace. "The issue," said a council member to the petitioner, "is whether or not the people in this community want to have their birds cease to tweet. I find it very difficult to understand the dichotomy here where you want to bring in an activity that would disrupt the kind of tranquility you yourself like."

And City Manager Rein says, "Our goal is to be able to retain what's here that people like and also allow the city to grow. That's a tough assignment, but we're optimistic about the future."

There is ample room for industry, light or heavy, in two public industrial parks and half a dozen private ones. A focal point for industrial development is the Bowers Hill area at the convergence of five highways.

Mary Bergey looks over the herd that produces milk for rich ice cream, a tradition at Bergey's Dairy Farm.

BILL TIERNAN

Chesapeake is also looking to the building of a major mall in the Western Branch area near the intersection of I-664 with Virginia Route 337.

In 1987, the Virginia General Assembly approved the creation of the Chesapeake Port Authority, which may acquire and develop land along Chesapeake's five-mile waterfront on the Elizabeth River's Southern Branch. Councilman John W. Butt foresaw "a great potential to be part of the Hampton Roads total port."

Each May, the city's birthday party, the Chesapeake Jubilee, draws 200,000 revelers. Reporter Judi Tull caught the startled expression on Mayor Oman's face when a balloon bore him skyward and the deadpan but watchful face of each youth parading cattle for the judges, the only sign of tension being the toe he or she dug in the dirt. Vocalist Chuck Berry rocked and rolled, thrill rides lifted large sections of the population to dizzying heights. The Vitale family's fireworks "lit up the nighttime sky with their three tons and $30,000 worth of beauty and boomers, set to the sounds of Sousa marches and Neil Diamond's 'America'. The grand finale spelled out WE THE PEOPLE in honor of the anniversary of the Constitution."

There's much to celebrate every day, starting with 58,000 acres of farmland, including Bergey's Dairy Farm, which still delivers milk in bottles and makes ice cream of 14 percent butterfat. At the Fentress Airfield, the Navy's fighter planes practice night landings on two areas painted to look like carrier decks. Remnants of the tribe of the Nansemond Indians elect their chiefs and crown them with bonnets. One may idle by the Great Bridge Lock and watch a procession of vessels pass through that key stop on the 1,500-mile Intracoastal Waterway. The Deep Creek Canal offers a scenic route that edges along the Dismal Swamp. Greenbrier Mall has an interior that makes one think of the opulent surroundings of Daddy Warbucks.

A favorite haunt is the 185-acre Northwest River Park, and, of course, there's a world of room in Old Dismal. Bolstered by gifts of swampland from Union Camp Corp. and Weyerhaeuser Co., the U.S. Department of the Interior rounded out the holdings to more than 100,000 acres, of which Virginia has 75 percent and North Carolina 25 percent. Within Virginia, Suffolk has a third and Chesapeake two-thirds of the swamp. About half as much again lies outside the refuge, and it is in that portion that hunting occurs. Headquarters for the refuge management is on Desert Road in Suffolk. (Natives pronounce desert as "de-sart," which was how William Byrd II spelled it in describing the swamp in his journal while running a boundary line in 1728 between the two states.) Other visitors have included George Washington, who helped form in 1763 the "Adventurers for Draining the Dismal Swamp" by digging canals. With a soldier's eye for terrain, Washington noted that Dismal was "neither plain nor a hollow but a hillside," with Lake Drummond, an amber jewel, at its highest point. In 1856, Harriet Beecher Stowe used it in

"Dred: A Slave of the Dismal Swamp." Irish poet Thomas Moore wrote in 1803 a ballad of a man searching for his lost love seen paddling about the swamp in a white canoe lit by a firefly lamp. Young poet Robert Frost visited the swamp's outskirts. Despondent at Miss Elinor White's rejection of a slim book of poems, Frost came from Boston with the idea of ending it all in Old Dismal, but instead he walked the Dismal Swamp Canal towpath to North Carolina and, much later, married Elinor. The swamp's main guise is impenetrability. From atop a fire tower, one gazes down at the thick canopy of trees as solid as if carved from green jade. And a person who ventures off a logging road even a few feet finds himself pushing in deep brush and silence. Guide Sam P. Whitson once explained, "You can't walk in a straight line because you have to follow the thin areas in getting around the undergrowth so that you constantly lose your sense of direction. You can get so confused in there you don't even believe your own compass. You have to pick out a landmark as far ahead as you can see, and then you may have to walk a half mile one way and a half mile back to get around a spot you couldn't cross. By the time you've walked three or five miles, you may have been turned in a direction that will be 20 miles from the nearest high land."

Three miles long and two miles wide, Lake Drummond lies in Virginia but is named for North Carolina's first governor, William Drummond. He was hanged in Jamestown, at the order of Virginia's Gov. Berkeley, for assisting Bacon's Rebellion. Its waters are tinted by juniper to a bourbon hue. At a nearby inn, the Halfway House straddling the border of the two states, a traveler mixed his drink at the bar and, mistaking the amber water for whiskey, kept cutting it from a decanter of clear gin, baffled that it grew stronger as he weakened it.

You won't find in the encyclopedia an entry on the Battle of Great Bridge, but it was the first pitched battle in the American Revolution and occurred after the Royal Governor, Lord Dunmore, fled Williamsburg for Norfolk. Had the patriots lost, the consequences would have been grave. "It was the most important battle in the first year of the war," says Judge Charles B. Cross Jr., who has written eight books about the City of Chesapeake he helped shape. On Dec. 9, 1775, at sunrise, coming from the direction of Norfolk, the British began attacking south six abreast along an earthen causeway across 360 yards of marsh and open water of the Southern Branch of the Elizabeth River. The patriots, 600 strong, waited behind breastworks at Great Bridge. The British had a regiment of the 14th Grenadiers and a couple of loyalist regiments raised in the

Silhouettes of reeds and birds on a golden background resemble a Chinese screen. Facing page: Just a few feet into the Dismal Swamp and the casual visitor can lose his bearings.

MARTIN RODDEN

Two girls soar skyward, upside down, in a thrill ride at the Jubilee, right. Pioneering rock 'n' roller Chuck Berry entertains crowd at the Jubilee, below.

At right, jampacked gondola lifts birthday party guests above Chesapeake. Facing page: An exploding star casts gaudy light over Chesapeake's birthday party.

area, and what Lord Dunmore called his Ethiopian Corps of slaves who had been promised their freedom. When the massed British troops were well within range, the patriots fired volleys into their ranks. There was no place to hide. Some 70 Britishers died. One American was wounded.

"It was amazing," said Judge Cross. "It was really a suicide attack. No military man in his right mind would have ordered it, but Dunmore was neither a military man nor in his right mind at the time. He had let the patriots drive him crazy, I guess." An American hero was Billy Flora, a free black from Portsmouth. At night he guarded stores on an island midway in the marsh. In the darkness before the dawn, when the British attacked, Flora stayed long enough to fire as many as eight times. "That takes a good while with a muzzle loader," Judge Cross said. Then Flora turned and ran for his life across the highway and into the breastworks. He lived in Portsmouth after the Revolution, and when he went down to volunteer in the War of 1812, he carried the same gun.

After the fight at Great Bridge, the British withdrew to Norfolk and two days later went aboard ships. They were confined there and couldn't regain a foothold in Virginia until 1779. Their absence enabled Virginia to use the Chesapeake Bay as the main artery in supplying Washington for five years. Before the Battle of Great Bridge, Washington had said that if Dunmore were not removed, the Royal Governor would gather forces like a snowball, divide the colonies, and doom the Revolution.

Patrick Henry, who had headed the patriot force at its formation in Williamsburg, left it after being elected Governor of Virginia. "You can see the larger place the battle would have had in history books if Henry had stayed in command," Judge Cross observed. Two other persons of interest, Thomas Marshall and his 19-year-old son, John, were at the battle. John Marshall stayed with Washington most of the way and emerged as a captain. "I went in the army a Virginian and became an American," he said. After the war, he stuck with Washington as a Federalist, as did most of the Founders who were with him during the war, opposing Thomas Jefferson's philosophy of states' rights. That period of John Marshall's education began at Great Bridge.

As you drive south along Battlefield Boulevard, nearing Great Bridge, you cross a small, barely noticeable bridge just short of a metal historic marker. Look to the left, and you catch a glimpse of the marsh, free of urban clutter, looking with its green reeds and marsh grass and blue winding waterways much as it was when Billy Flora fired his musket at invading redcoats.

Of all Chesapeake's amenities, which is most vital? "Our schools," replied Vice Mayor Willa Bazemore. "We pay individual attention to all situations. Parents come at any time to discuss any matter on the well-being of their children. Our dropout rate is among the lowest in the United States because we use many ways to keep students in school."

BILL PORTLOCK

MARTIN RODDEN

One more vessel passes through the Great Bridge Lock,
a key stop on the Intracoastal Waterway, top. Chief Earl Running
Deer Bass places ceremonial bonnet on the head of William Strong
Bear Langston, a new assistant chief, bottom.

Below, Greenbrier Mall's four-story atrium offers antiques among its changing shows. At the Navy's Fentress airfield, an F-14 Tomcat touches down on an area painted to resemble a carrier deck, left.

97

Eastern Shore

Residents of Virginia's Eastern Shore, a peninsula hanging from Maryland like a Christmas stocking, depended for centuries on a ferry to reach the mother mainland. Isolation fostered a sense of independence that persisted even after the opening of the Chesapeake Bay Bridge-Tunnel in 1964. Not long ago a caller on Virginia's mainland telephoned Accomack County and asked if he could speak to an official there. No, his secretary said, he wouldn't return from a trip until the next day. "He's out of the state, in Richmond," she said.

God blessed the Shore by laving it on the east with the Atlantic Ocean and on the west with the Chesapeake Bay. The waters insulate the 72-mile strip and assure a mild climate for harvesting seafood and growing grains, fruits, and vegetables in sandy loam. It is a Garden of Eden.

Under the push of a hurricane, the ocean can act up, but the big winds bring sweet rains and the watermen know how to ride out a storm. When hardy ones still clung to barrier islands in the ocean, tidal waves smacked the beaches and washed over communities. Hog Island's residents opened front and back doors and let the ocean roar in one door and out the other. Otherwise, it would have carried the house away. Life on the Shore can be profoundly simple.

People, too, tend to be forthright. Take waterman Will Melvin, who declined to take Cap'n Polk Lang's fishing boat to the pounds during high water. Lang retorted that he would ask his wife, Nan, to fish the pounds. Will, irked at that, agreed to take out the boat. When the pair reached Metompkin Inlet, Cap'n Polk, seeing breakers rolling in from the ocean, ordered Will to turn around. Will kept heading straight for the bar. Cap'n Polk picked up a hammer, but Will took it away and threw it overboard. The first breaker picked up the boat, tossed it skyward, and dropped it in the following trough, splitting it in two. The Coast Guard rescued them.

In the hurricane of 1933, boats were wrecked, sunk, or cast ashore. When Cap'n Polk couldn't find Will, he put out a boat and started out Folly Creek looking for Will's body. Reaching the creek's mouth, he saw a man tonging for oysters. It was Will.

"Will, you fool, why didn't you come ashore?" Polk asked.

A boy watches from the pier as a Midas sun turns the water to gold.

Will kept tonging. "I had enough gas," he said. "I threw over a couple of anchors, kept her nose to the breeze, and kept her motor going. As soon as the storm was over, I went to work." Will Melvin, among other independent watermen, may be found in L. Floyd Nock II's little book, "What the Saturday Evening Post Missed."

Once in a great while rugged individualism becomes eccentricity, which the residents accept as just another manifestation of human nature. At a lane's end in a field off Route 13 is the site of the estate of Arlington. In the family graveyard lies John Custis IV, who died, the tombstone says: "Aged 71 years/ and yet liv'd but Seven Years which/ was the span of time He kept a Batchelers house at Arlington on the Eastern Shore of/ Virginia."

Col. Custis and his wife, Frances, were strong-willed, forever quarreling, and decided to speak only through a slave, Pompey. The Colonel invited his wife for a drive, but after going a short distance across the hard-packed sand, he drove the horse into the Bay.

"Where are you going, Col. Custis?" she asked.

"To hell, Madam!" he retorted.

"Drive on," she said. "Anything is better than Arlington!"

He turned to shore. "Madam," he said, "I believe you would as lief meet the Devil himself if I should drive to hell."

"Quite true, sir," she said, "I know you so well I would not be afraid to go anywhere you would go."

The Shore has its architecture, known as "big house-little house-colonnade-and-kitchen," four parts strung out like a child's blocks. In Colonial times as a family grew, the house grew with it, part by part. The style persists with many of today's houses, no matter their cost or size.

The Eastern Shore depends on three crops: seafood, produce, tourists. Visitors stroll through the old towns, watch birds, attend the annual pony penning when watermen put on high rubber boots and become cow-boys. They round up wild ponies on Assateague Island, herd them across the channel to Chincoteague Island, and auction them to help the volunteer fire department. Nobody knows when ponies came to Assateague. Some say they swam ashore from a Spanish galleon that wrecked in the 16th century, others that the settlers hid their steeds on Assateague in 1662 to escape a tax on horses. Ask a 'teaguer, and he will shrug his shoulders and say, "It was long before moi toime."

During April, there's the Weekend of the Islands when watermen exhibit handicrafts and demonstrate the art of carving birds and beasts. On the first Wednesday in May comes the Eastern Shore Annual Seafood Festival, so popular that tickets are sold out the preceding September.

With 105,000 acres of farmland and 114,000 acres in timber, the Eastern Shore is a cornucopia of fruits, vegetables, and grains. In the 1930s, there were 3,000

farms, ranging from 50 to 75 acres; by 1982, there were 415 farms, many of the corporate variety. From 2,200 acres, tilled by only four producers, come tomatoes that grossed $27 million. Marketing methods changed also — and to the farmers' disadvantage. Formerly Route 13 had been dotted with stalls with produce for sale. There were numerous auction blocks at which middlemen bid for crops. During the 1950s, buyers began working by telephone and competition dwindled with the auction blocks. The last auction was in the mid-1960s in Exmore. With prices dropping on corn and soybeans in the mid-1980s, a move started among farmers to shift from low-value grains and return to an emphasis on high-value truck crops. Farm groups also were studying ways to update marketing and establish a farmers market to assure better profits for the growers.

The Eastern Shore is tethered to Virginia via the 17.6-mile Chesapeake Bay Bridge-Tunnel. Financed by a $200 million bond issue, backed by tolls, it required 37 months to build. It bends its way across the Bay this way and that, under and over the water, like a rudely articulated toy snake. Removal of the $9 toll, probably about the year 2000, will release a land rush into the Shore from the Virginia mainland while rapid growth is coming from Maryland and Delaware. The Shore will be in the path of a pincer of development that could change its character radically. A stabilizing factor is the non-profit Nature Conservancy. From Brownsville it tends 35,000 acres of a dozen barrier islands and their rookeries of herons, and other waterbirds and wintering grounds for geese, swans, and ducks. The slim, shifting islands are pit stops on the migratory corridor for clouds of hawks and other birds. In the long stretch of fragile barriers along the nation's East Coast, only those off Virginia are without human habitation.

In February 1985, the Conservancy acquired 6,200 acres on the Eastern Shore from the Allegheny Duck Club of Pittsburgh, which had spent eight years buying property in Northampton and Accomack counties along 50 miles of coast from below Cape Charles almost to Wallops Island. In a unique program, the Conservancy began marketing large tracts with guidelines to protect woods, wetlands, and waterways, encourage good farming practices, create buffers for ecologically fragile spots, and assure a low density of dwellings. Development of coastal bays, the Conservancy thinks, would destroy the islands' ecosystem that is a spawning ground for fish, a sea larder for the Shore's fishing industry.

"You couldn't lock up the sea side from any kind of economic growth," said the Conservancy's L. Gregory Low, "but the program should please everybody by adding to the tax base, protecting assets on which farmers and watermen depend, saving habitats of wildlife, and preserving the incredible resource of the bays that scallop the peninsula."

At left, Dunlin sandpipers blur the sky over a beach on the Eastern Shore.

BILL PORTLOCK

101

At right, a Tangier man pushes a bicycle into the dawn. With the Chesapeake Bay Bridge-Tunnel in the background, a boy walks the beach at sunset, below.

MICHELE MCDONALD

RAYMOND GEHMAN

At right, distinctive style marks growth of Eastern Shore families and houses. Facing page: Dappled ponies emerge from a channel swim at Chincoteague.

L. FLOYD NOCK

Norfolk

Norfolk keeps coming back. Few other American cities suffered as much from war, pestilence, and depression. None is more resilient. It was founded in 1680 on 50 acres at the mouth of the Elizabeth River's Eastern Branch. As English ships grew in size and had trouble reaching plantation wharfs along creeks, Norfolk became their dock.

By the Revolutionary War, its population was 6,000, half that of New York. But on Jan. 1, 1776, the warships of Lord Dunmore, the royal governor who had fled from Williamsburg, bombarded the town. The cannonading punched holes in a few buildings; sorties ashore destroyed 19 homes. When the British returned to their ships, the Colonial troops turned to burning Norfolk, eliminating it as a British base. In three days they destroyed 863 buildings. Abandoning the town in February, they torched the remaining 416. All that was left of Norfolk were the walls of St. Paul's Church.

Set now amid magnolias, hemmed in by sleek urban renewal, Old St. Paul's has a Dunmore cannonball lodged in its east wall, a shot in the craw typifying the city's gritty destiny. The ball, after striking St. Paul's in 1776, had dropped to the ground. Citizens mortised it into a dent. For years a sign pointed TO THE CANNONBALL. A little to the right, and it would have missed the church — and a place in the Norfolk Tour.

After the war, Norfolk welcomed English and Scottish merchants who came over to set up shop. The city was climbing out of ruins when fire again destroyed much of it in 1799 and 1804. Outbreak of war in Europe in 1792 boosted American shipping and Norfolk's recovery, but Jefferson's embargo of 1807 and the War of 1812 reduced exports to a trickle. After that war, cities at the fall line blocked efforts to extend railroads to Norfolk.

Yellow fever scourged it in 1795, 1802, and 1821. Only the frost in 1855 broke the pestilence that took 2,000 lives. From that ordeal, the city plunged into the Civil War and suffered occupation under Gen. Benjamin F. "Beast" Butler. After the war half a dozen railroads reached the area.

In 1907, 300 years after settlers arrived at Cape Henry, Norfolk produced the Tercentennial Jamestown Exposition. Hampered by rains, the show wasn't fully mounted until September, but it drew international notice to the city's grand harbor, and the Navy acquired the exposition grounds on a splendid waterfront as the site for the world's largest naval base, just in time for it to become a staging area for ships ferrying doughboys

Clouds suds the blue sky, ships speckle the river in a view of Waterside on the Norfolk skyline.

to Europe in World War I.

Every so often the city is revitalized, as it was after World War I in adopting the city manager form of government and hiring Charles E. Ashburner, who had been, in Staunton, Va., the nation's first city manager. He saw that the city had first-rate services. Another strong manager, Maj. I. Walke Truxton, was described by "The City Manager" as having "a high-strung tenacity coupled with a high ideal of public service." He energized police, improved health services, upgraded schools, built a surplus.

City Manager Thomas P. Thompson, arriving in 1933, sought federal aid to cushion the Depression. The notion took some getting used to, but soon the Council accepted Washington's help in building bridges and schools, expanding the art museum and the airport, and funding in 1936 the planting of a botanical garden to create jobs for 200 women. Thompson hired gardener Frederic C. Heutte, a French transplant, son of a coachman and an American girl who had gone to Paris to learn dressmaking. The city manager and the gardener roamed the city as one great garden. Heutte knocked on doors along Ballentine Boulevard inviting homeowners to plant a parade of crape myrtles. The idea took root and spread. In July and August, nodding plumes of pink, lavender, red, and white line the streets. The 200 WPA workers called ruddy-faced, gnarled-featured Heutte "flower man." Clubwomen dubbed him "King Gardener" and stormed the chamber when the Council cut garden funds. It restored the funds and Heutte served 30 years beautifying the city. Every April the Azalea Festival is in Botanical Gardens with a Queen and a court from nations in NATO.

When urban renewal erased relics of the old waterfront, the housing authority saved a charming pavilion at the ferry terminal and relocated it in Ghent Square. In 1980, the Friends of Fred Heutte transformed it into a center relating gardens to the arts. The Friends installed an herb knot garden, which would have pleased Heutte. Wherever he went, he carried a penknife and brought back cuttings in damp tissues. Anything, he said, grows in Hampton Roads, warmed by the Gulf Stream and in a climatic zone blending Spanish moss and evergreens.

Shipyard workers and sailors doubled Norfolk's population during World War II. The city obtained federal help for housing, hospitals, roads. When the Federal War Agency allocated $278,000 for a temporary recreation center, City Manager Charles B. Borland demanded a lasting one. The city added $245,000, and the agency agreed to a permanent center with a 2,000-seat auditorium and a 5,000-seat arena, the country's largest USO building for its greatest concentration of troops. It still serves, with opera emoting at one end, wrestlers at the other.

The Depression and a cutback in Naval forces hit Norfolk hard. Alarmed at the crime problem, Borland appointed in 1935 a five-man study committee (headed

KAREN D. TWIDDY

KATHY DIX

WILLIAM ABOURJILIE

Clockwise from above: Just at dusk, dressed in lights, Scope Cultural and Convention Center is a show itself. Crystalline splendor marks the Virginia Opera's production of "The Merry Widow." Music echoes among buildings as Winston Dan Vogel leads the Virginia Symphony in MacArthur Square. The newly expanded Chrysler Museum houses a treasure trove at the head of The Hague.

KAREN D. TWIDDY (2)

by Charles L. Kaufman) which documented that slums bred crime and poverty. It urged their elimination. In 1938, 350 persons met in a junior high school and decided to try once more the Community Chest drive that had failed 13 of 15 years. It succeeded ever after.

World War II nearly split the city's seams. War's end found Norfolk slum-ridden, burdened with a scandal-tainted police force. Civic leaders backed three businessmen for the City Council — J. Pretlow Darden, Richard D. Cooke, and John Twohy II — who campaigned in 1946 for reform. They vowed to retire after one term. Norfolk began solving problems five to 10 years before most U.S. cities came to grips with similar ones. The Council risked $25,000 for a study of how to use federal aid rumored to be in the offing. A year later in 1949, Norfolk won the nation's first urban renewal grant.

It hired C.A. Harrell from Schenectady, N.Y., as city manager and assured him that Council members had no friends to be favored. The Council created a port authority, expanded the water system, and cleared 1,000 acres of slums. "Our goal was to try to improve the level of the people we were trying to house," said Kaufman, chairman of redevelopment and housing. Some who moved into the authority's low-rent housing had "the first real bath in their lives," he noted. In one building, 150 families had lived in 150 rooms with six toilets and six spigots. Slum properties had produced net returns up to 40 percent. Their elimination met stiff resistance, former Housing Director Lawrence M. Cox recalled. When a woman raged at a Council session that she'd get even with Darden next election, the mayor asked if she had voted for him in the previous one.

"No," she replied.

"Then you missed your only opportunity to vote for me," Darden said.

The drive for reforms persisted four decades under effective councils and city managers. An abiding problem was how to revive the downtown core when shoppers deserted it for suburban malls. In 1965, Norfolk's business leaders hired developer James W. Rouse to lure a major department store to 17 acres adjacent to Granby Street, downtown's lifeline. The effort failed. The search continued.

Norfolk built a civic center, including the City Hall, overlooking the Elizabeth River. The view proved irresistible. The region's banks built headquarters there, anchoring Norfolk as the financial center. Former Mayor Roy B. Martin Jr. used to say that Darden's administration plowed the ground, Mayor Fred Duckworth's sowed the seed, and Martin's brought in the sheaves. Through Thomas Maxwell's shrewd management, Norfolk could supply funds to qualify for urban renewal, "which was the city's rebirth," Martin said.

Duckworth led in turning Norfolk's old Courthouse into a memorial for Gen. Douglas MacArthur. The Captain was buried in the Naval town because his mother had been born there. MacArthur just missed

From atop the Dominion Tower, Norfolk seems to be gift-wrapped and trimmed in ribbons of light at Christmas.

Norfolk's skyline along the waterfront is limned in Christmas lights beneath a star burst from a rocket.

being a native son when his father was transferred to an army post in Little Rock, Ark. "It was in-tended that I be born in Virginia," the general said sonorously, disposing of Little Rock's bid to be his resting place. The main building, along with an auditorium and a research center, fills a little square over which the general's bronze statue presides. Its galleries are as packed with MacArthur's memorabilia (including corncob pipe, sunglasses, visored cap) as a soldier's foot locker.

Designed in Greek Revival by William Singleton of Portsmouth, it has a cupola that falls just short of being a full-bosomed dome. Thomas U. Walter, who designed the nation's Capitol dome, was the consultant. Observed on Norfolk's skyline, the quaint oyster-gray courthouse, silhouetted with its modest yet distinctive cupola against the gleaming cash boxes of banks, is a quiet touch with the past. The square has become a site for festivities. The Virginia Symphony plays there, music reverberating among skyscrapers.

The MacArthur Memorial's soul, the research center, brings together scholars for international seminars, as when Beate Sirota Gordon, describing her work as a young woman during the postwar occupation of Japan, told how a committee shaped a constitution that in-cluded, at her behest, an equal rights amendment.

When Jean Outland Chrysler, a Norfolk native, mentioned in 1971 to Mayor Martin that her husband, Walter P. Chrysler Jr., needed a home for his paintings, then in Provincetown, Mass., Martin convened 15 civic leaders to confer with Chrysler. The city received a trove of art and the Norfolk Museum of Arts and Sciences became the Chrysler Museum of Norfolk, ranked among the nation's top 20 museums.

Swift action also ensued when Cox learned in Washington, D.C., that a bill in the Senate would fund a cultural and convention center for Denver, Colo. Next morning Martin announced that Norfolk would build such a center. Sen. A. Willis Robertson tagged Norfolk to the Denver bill, and Rep. Porter Hardy Jr. labored a week to save the amendment in a conference commit-tee. Norfolk received Scope, a $37 million center and concert hall to which the city contributed $10 million. It is a lovely curve on the skyline, half a sphere exposed. Approaching it, the visitor sees a patch of the dome with something of the excitement at the first glimpse of a weather-bleached circus tent shining in the sun. Sup-ports, attached to the outer walls, are fashioned like giant ropes seeming to tie down the tent.

Norfolk lured City Manager G. Robert House from Chesapeake. He brought with him the professionalism and the courage for innovative solutions that he also practiced later as city manager in Suffolk and in Portsmouth until his death, with three aides, in an airplane crash while they were on a civic mission. His gifts enriched the region.

Norfolk still looked for a way to revive the downtown. In that period, former City Manager C.A. Harrell returned for a civic banquet in his honor. He com-

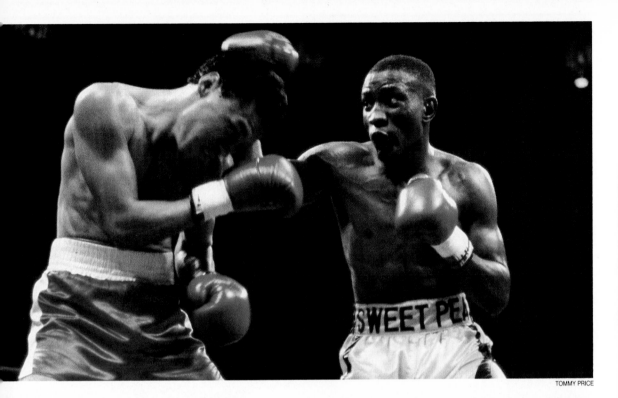

TOMMY PRICE

MICHELE McDONALD

At left, Norfolk's Sweetpea Whitaker continues carving his career on malleable material. Below, Old Dominion University's Monarchs habitually schedule tough opponents.

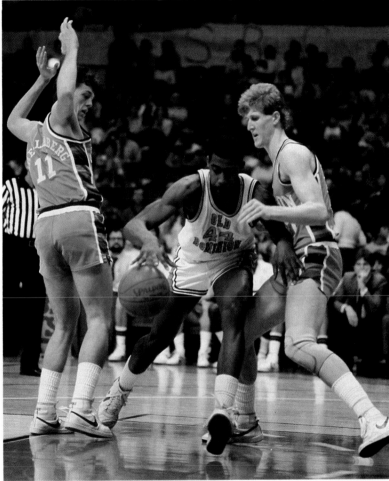

RAYMOND GEHMAN

Norfolk State University's Spartans, the class of their league, draw record crowds, left. Facing page: Contenders in the Elizabeth River Run throng the Hampton Boulevard Bridge.

At right, which is more alluring, the pottery or the putterer at Ghent Art Festival? In the parade for the Azalea Festival, the NATO country of Turkey presents a princess, below.

MICHELE McDONALD

JOHN H. SHEALLY II

An appealing spectacle at the Scottish Festival is a deadpan spectator, right. Facing page: Fireworks lend luster to the crowded waterfront at Waterside during Harborfest.

LOIS BERNSTEIN

mended the city's willingness to experiment and act boldly. "But remember," he said, "that in any experiment there are two kinds of guinea pigs, those that die and those that live. Be sure that Norfolk is among the latter."

A test arose with the proposed Norfolk Gardens, an elaborate landscape under glass, but projected costs soared and in Mayor Irvine B. Hill's administration, the Council balked at the price and that dream faded.

"In 1978, things had ground to a halt," said Dr. Mason C. Andrews, one of several civic leaders who formed Greater Norfolk Corp. with the idea that the private sector working with government could find solutions. The group met weekly. In 1979, several conferred with developer Rouse, who was vacationing with his Norfolk-born wife, Patty, at Sandbridge. He had already embarked on a new course of creating festival markets, and he agreed to try again in Norfolk, touched at their patience and faith after the initial failure. "Mason was particularly persistent," he recalled.

Saltwater runs like blood in Norfolk's veins, and now, through a festival place named Waterside, the city found its way back to the banks of the Elizabeth River where it had started. Waterside's architecture drew on the design of the original little ferry pavilion that had been moved to Ghent Square. The night Waterside opened, Norfolkians unconsciously quickened their pace as they sighted the light-fringed pavilion. They crowded its two stories and its grand staircases and thronged the promenades by the water. It was a gigantic reception, with smiling City Manager Julian F. Hirst and Mayor Vincent J. Thomas. For the mayor it was a second triumph. He had worked as School Board chairman to uphold the school system's quality. Here and there were frequent rushes through the crowd as old friends sighted each other, after long absence, back downtown. Amid it all stood Andrews, shaking hands, a grin on his face. To continue Waterside's success as a magnet, Karen Scherberger and her team organize fest-events 150 days a year as well as major celebrations, such as Harborfest. At Christmas the city's buildings are trimmed in ribbands of light and the skyline of towering blocks is edged in flame.

The city's growth is urgent as new Ghent and watergirt condominiums fill vacant lands. Restaurants crowd the fringes of downtown so that the core's salvation, it appears, will come from without as well as from within. Norfolk, as City Manager James B. Oliver observed, is self-made, largely, grappling problems much more severe than those affecting many communities. "Leaders from business, churches, and neighborhoods come forward to ask what they can do," he noted.

"Individuals are willing to come together to try to solve problems and eliminate difficulties as opposed to looking for confrontation and their own self-interest," Mayor Joseph A. Leafe said. "An underlying spirit wants the city to do well, and it creates the pride that makes a difference."

113

Virginia Beach

GLEN McCLURE

If Odysseus had stopped at Virginia Beach, he would have never made it home to Penelope. The sand and sea are so seductive. It's as if the beach has been spread there for your benefit, a wide, unending, beige couch on which you can flop, walk, run. Oh, technically, an owner's property probably extends to the waterline, but the raising of a barrier would be regarded as heinous. Emanations of felt disapproval would beat against it. Virginia Beach is widely regarded as the hospitable front doorstep of Virginia.

From the southern edge of False Cape Park, moving north past the hotels on the beach front and taking the turn west into the Chesapeake Bay all the way to Little Creek Naval Amphibious Base there is a 38-mile-long belt of sand. If you continue west into Norfolk's Ocean View Beach, along the Chesapeake Bay, to the Hampton Roads Bridge Tunnel, there are 45 miles of sand.

And ocean, tumbling, running, as many as seven waves reaching back toward the horizon, tossing white manes as they race toward shore. Those white-foaming waves rushing the shore bring to mind Rosa Bonheur's painting of the Horse Fair, white horses swirling.

After being rolled around by combers, you run to fall on the sand and, with the sea's susurrus in the background, you snooze under the sun's blessing. A half hour on the beach can change your perspective from harried to languid. One just doesn't care any more about whatever was driving one a few minutes before the sea's embrace. The sea is Circe.

When friends move from other localities to the Beach, you might as well kiss 'em goodbye. You never see 'em again, at least not in Norfolk or Suffolk or other places that suddenly become remote to their minds. Visit them two or three times in Virginia Beach, and when you press them to come to Norfolk, they grow vague, their eyes become abstract. They mumble something about it's too far to Norfolk and it's all uphill, as if the Blue Ridge Mountains reared their ramparts between Norfolk and Virginia Beach.

Of course, some residents among the thickly populated subdivisions just don't get around to going to the beach, but there's the sense of its being there — a scent of brine in the air and the sight of a Volkswagen scurrying along the toll road with a surfboard mounted on the roof. In mind's eye is a scene of two dozen youths,

Hotels and motels, ornate as sand castles, line the oceanfront, where vacationers play, at Virginia Beach.

At left, a single surfer has an orange sky and the Atlantic Ocean all to himself. Facing page: Athletes seeking to win the triathlon crown at the Neptune Festival prepare to test their strength against the ocean.

All a boy could ask for on the beach: blue sky, water, and a bogie board.

RAYMOND GEHMAN (2)

piling out of cars onto the beach at 44th Street, the girls advancing sedately across the incline of the broad sands, the boys running, flinging off shoes, shirts, jeans as they go, scattering them across the sand, and diving into the crashing, tingling white surf.

With a population of 360,000 increasing as much as 2,000 a month, Virginia Beach is the state's largest, fastest growing city. The borough of Kempsville with 80,000 residents is pressing the City of Roanoke, the state's eighth largest city with its 100,000. A "green line" — running down Princess Anne Road (starting at Tidewater Community College) and extending to the rows of cottages by the ocean at Sandbridge — divides the city into a highly developed populous northern half of subdivisions and malls and a largely rural southern half of rustling corn. Much of the southern half sits in a flood plain of both water and population, and there is a mounting feeling among the people and their government that the two shouldn't be allowed to mix.

For a quarter of a century after the birth of modern Virginia Beach, there was no downtown, no markedly discernible center. In the mid-1980s, two began to emerge, one among office buildings sprouting around Pembroke Mall a few miles from Norfolk's boundary, the other around the city hall complex, outsized Colonial-style buildings at old Princess Anne Courthouse on the verge of the southern half. They are, roughly, two poles, urban and rural, a dichotomy that reflects the personality of the city when it was born in 1963 with the merger of the two-square mile resort City of Virginia Beach and the vast farming County of Princess Anne, a tadpole swallowing a frog. The man who managed this remarkable transmogrification was affable, easygoing, highly pragmatic, and, when need be, unyielding, Sidney S. Kellam, chief of the Democratic organization at Virginia Beach and a lieutenant to Harry F. Byrd Sr.

When the campaigns of Byrd-blessed candidates for governor were "in trouble," word went out to "call Sidney." As with any request, Kellam would say, "I'll see what I can do," — and then go to the candidate's headquarters at the Hotel Richmond and live with the campaign until it was done. Asked once what he liked best about politics, Kellam replied, "Winning." But he was a gracious compromiser. "My backup gear is just as good as my forward gear," he said. "I've had to eat crow so often it tastes like turkey." Such modest self-appraisals also had the effect of disarming the other parties to a deal. To the disgust of some of his aides, he was generous with former foes who returned to the fold. There is a story, probably apocryphal, that Abel Kellam used to sit Sidney and his 11 brothers by the road to the Princess Anne County Courthouse and instruct them to speak to everybody.

With great elan, Walter Noona conducts the Virginia Beach Pops, left. Facing page: The sun also sets at Virginia Beach, reflected in the arches of the Pavilion.

Sidney Kellam, who was county treasurer 20 years, is hailed as "the father of modern Virginia Beach." In January 1960, a year after Norfolk annexed 13.5 square miles of Princess Anne County and seemed likely to take another bite, Kellam went to the Norfolk City Council and proposed that a study focus on a merger of all southside Hampton Roads cities and counties into one government of boroughs. And he promised not to seek any changes in state law limiting a city's right to annex if Norfolk would agree not to annex any part of Princess Anne County for five years. The metro study began, with Kellam as chairman.

Meanwhile, at the State Capitol, laws on consolidation of localities were being liberalized, and on Sept. 13, 1961, 17 months after Kellam's metro proposal, Princess Anne County and Virginia Beach officials disclosed that a merger of their localities was in the works. Kellam's forces waged practically a door-to-door campaign seeking the voters' approval of the merger. A threat by Norfolk Mayor Fred Duckworth to cut off the water to Norfolk's neighbors — "hold a water pistol to our head," Kellam said — simply enhanced the merger's chances and it carried handily. The resort city and the county came together tongue-on-groove in the charter presented to the General Assembly. In selecting a name, Kellam persuaded his Princess Anne brethren that if the new city weren't named Virginia Beach, the resort area would suffer severe economic losses because nobody would associate Princess Anne with the Atlantic Ocean. The merger under Norfolk's nose was a political coup that produced a new city of 310 square miles and stimulated similar mergers of South Norfolk and Norfolk County into the City of Chesapeake and of Suffolk and Nansemond into the City of Suffolk. Abel's affable son had set forces in motion that changed the map of southside Hampton Roads.

He died at 83. The Nimmo United Methodist Church could hold only 200 mourners. Hundreds stood outside surrounded by a sea of automobiles. A latecomer, driving under the trees, was waved into a parking place by a former Princess Anne County functionary. As the grateful driver climbed out of his car, the official said, "We look after our friends."

The Virginia Marine Science Museum had its beginning because there was no storage closet large enough at Cox High School for teacher Don Ives' rock collection. He reported to School Superintendent Edward E. Brickell that the system needed a science research room. Brickell appointed a committee which recommended a nature center that eventually evolved into a museum, which cost $8.5 million: $4.5 million from the state, $2 million from the city, $2 million from individuals. Its ingenious exhibits focus on the fauna and flora of the Chesapeake Bay. It simply is a whale of a museum.

It has 350 fish, give or take 25 or so, and 100 buttons that activate educational exhibits. Among the most popular is a carpeted platform on which children can

use a token, resembling a fiddler crab, to push a marble along a track through a maze tracing the crab's day. At the first fork is a choice between confronting a mullet or a croaker. If the child goes the way of the mullet, the crab proceeds unharmed to the next challenge. If the choice is the croaker, the marble drops into a hole that stands for the croaker's maw, and the child begins the game again. In a year the worn carpet has had to be replaced thrice.

At the top end of the scale of the 110 exhibits is a 50,000-gallon aquarium extending 125 feet along a slanting passage. It is a living, shifting, brilliantly colored mural of the world beneath the sea. The tank's habitat in the darkened corridor resembles the depths around the barnacled footings of pillars supporting the Chesapeake Bay Bridge-Tunnel.

For nature in the wild, Virginia Beach has diverse settings. In the remote southeastern portion of the city is 4,000-acre False Cape State Park, a strip of land between the Atlantic Ocean and Back Bay. Public transportation is nil. One must go five miles by bike, boat, or foot. But it is worth the effort. Bay, forest, beach grass, and beach all occur within half a mile. The visitor may come upon otters, muskrats, deer, wild pigs, and marsh rabbits, dark brown, with no cotton tail. When pressed, the marsh rabbit will take to the water.

Abutting False Cape Park is Back Bay National Wildlife Refuge, a haven for bird watchers as well as birds. At the other end of Virginia Beach is the 2,770-acre Seashore State Park, one of the oldest and the most popular in the state's system. Here and there are ponds, fringed with cypress trees knee-deep in water like plumbers struggling to plug a leak. Now that the pesticide DDT has been banned and the eagles have returned, a visitor occasionally sights that regal bird over Back Bay or off the coast of the seaside portion of the park. There are no thrill rides, no stage shows or rock groups, no places to eat or buy gifts, but a million persons jog or walk through Seashore State Park every year. It should be a reminder to officialdom of the value in setting aside portions of wilderness where individuals may re-create themselves.

And when it comes to restoring one's soul, there's the Virginia Beach Boardwalk Art Show, sponsored by the Virginia Beach Arts Center, which is the only institution in Hampton Roads to focus solely on 20th century American artists. The Boardwalk Art Show, attended by 350,000, is one of the largest outdoor art shows in the country. It began in 1956 and has climbed steadily in popularity. The gallery is, literally, as big as all outdoors. For five days in mid-July, it spreads paintings, prints, drawings, sculpture 10 blocks along the cement boardwalk between the motels and the beach.

A knowledgeable buyer may take home bargains, and, for the general spectator, it is a tossup as to which

In a soft light, a row of catamarans looks like bright butterflies on the sand.

In an early-morning walk at Back Bay, something catches a bird watcher's interest, right. A man, with his dog, poles a hunting skiff in the Back Bay Wildlife Refuge, below.

At right, golden sunlight bathes spectators on walkway in the marsh at Back Bay. Facing page: At the water's edge, a child stoops to pick up a shell and casts a foot-to-foot reflection.

Chick's Beach, on Chesapeake Bay, draws a multitude of the young, left. A stern visage of Neptune, cast in sand, gazes over his domain during his festival, below.

A cluster of catamarans gathers at Chick's Beach for the benevolent Low Rent Regatta, above.

is the more diverting, the art or the persons gazing at it. The blue sky is like a broad canvas, and the dazzling sun sweeps the scene like a paint brush, heightening the colors, highlighting the shapes. If the artist, relaxing in a canvas chair, finds that sales are slow, he or she can run to the shore, plunge under the tingling salt-ladened surf and wash frustrations away, come back revived and study the individuals looking at the art.

And smack on the boardwalk at 24th Street is the Virginia Beach Maritime Historical Museum. It used to be the old Seatack life-saving station. It opened in 1981 after a grass-roots campaign to save the historic building from destruction. It tells the story of the life-saving station and has changing exhibitions as well. It offers a welcome respite should the bright beach scene become too much.

There is growing awareness among the people and their legislators of the need to protect some of the very amenities that draw settlers to Virginia Beach. Forecasts indicate that within 30 to 40 years the Beach population will have nearly doubled to 500,000, which is about half the count now of the people in the seven major cities around Hampton Roads. Sidney Kellam himself — and he was a Realtor — once remarked of unplanned growth: "With all the land we have, I think it's a shame that we're allowing houses to be built on such small lots. The houses are so close that when you put your fist out the window you can punch your neighbor in the face. I think building on such small lots has a tendency to make blighted areas more quickly."

The forest in Seashore State Park carpets 25,000-year-old ridges. At the very north end of the beach, behind the streets numbering into the 80s, are 30-foot-high living dunes, hills and deep bowls of sand, bare except for fringes of brush, still moving and shaping themselves, inch by inch as the wind blows sand up the gentler slope and drops it on the advancing face of the dune. In 1970, the state yielded to pressure from the city and leased 15 acres of the giant dunes as the site for a school, although there was ample space elsewhere. Citizens persuaded the state to reverse its decision.

The dunes are a block or so from a granite cross marking the area on Cape Henry where the colonists landed in 1607. The dunes are about now as they were then. John Smith may have walked them in his zestful exploration of what was to become Hampton Roads. In his sensitivity to everything about him — animals, Indians, rivers, trees — and his scorn for his fellows "who never adventured to know anything," he resembled many today, among persons of all ages and walks of life who wish to retain something of what is distinctive in the wondrous world of Hampton Roads.

At right, two appreciative fishermen pause to watch the sun set at Back Bay. Center: A fisherman cleans his catch on a pier at Virginia Beach against a sky aflame. Far right: Swimmers and surfers frolic against a backdrop in red at Virginia Beach.

MICHELE McDONALD

To see infinity in a grain of sand and in a child at play at Ocean View. . . .

The writer is grateful to The Virginian-Pilot and The Ledger-Star for a generous contribution toward the publication of this book and to Randy Jessee, assistant to the executive editor, for help throughout the project. He also enjoyed working with the Future of Hampton Roads' publications committee: Dale Bowen, Thomas P. Chisman, Henry Clay Hofheimer II, and William D. Wilkinson.

In Newport News, the Daily Press and The Times-Herald opened their photographic files. To requests for help, Jim Livengood, manager of the newspapers' photographic department, complied with unfailing good humor, as did the other photographers, and librarians Theresa Hammond, Karen Booth-Opel, and Earl Riggins III.

In Norfolk, graphics director Bob Lynn and chief photographer William Abourjilie made available the newspapers' color slides, and they and the other photographers and secretary Mary Holliday took a zestful interest in the work. The newspapers' librarians — Ann Johnson, Clara Basnight, Peggy Deans, Marvin Elder, Kim Kent, Tara Martin, Diana Cramer, and Maureen Watts — helped, as did WHRO-TV's Tim Morton.

Others helpful were Debbie Carson-Gorman of the Virginia Port Authority, Constance Rhodes of the Isle of Wight/Smithfield Chamber of Commerce, Judith E. Braband of the Gloucester County Chamber of Commerce, Elsa Cooke of the Gazette-Journal of Gloucester, Margaret D. Porterfield of the Eastern Shore of Virginia Tourism Commission, Mary Nimmo of the Virginia Division of Tourism, Sylvia Weinstein of the Virginia Peninsula Economic Development Council, Deborah Wakefield of the Norfolk Convention and Visitors Bureau, Terri Walter and Gallon Tothero of CBN University, David Shufflebarger of Old Dominion University, Paulo Delo of Christopher Newport College, Mary Bruner of Virginia Wesleyan College.

Also, Joseph Stutts of Union Camp Corp., Judy Childress of the Veterans Administration Medical Center, June McPartland of the City of Hampton, Mindy Hughes of the City of Chesapeake, Karen Warren of the City of Suffolk, Margaret Jones and Miriam Francis of Suffolk, Elaine Bradbury of Poquoson, Debra M. Darr of Norfolk, Suzanne Brown and Sandy Belan of Colonial Williamsburg, Carol Wilbern of the Casemate Museum, Andrea Deveikis of the Virginia Living Museum, Belle Pendleton of the APVA, Verne Edwards of Smithfield, Adrienne Combs of Fort Eustis, Ross Weeks and Debby Padgett of the Jamestown-Yorktown Foundation, Arthur Polizos Associates Inc. and its Charles Applebach, and Seamark Inc. for lending slides.

Also, Parke Rouse Jr. of Williamsburg, Alexander Crosby Brown of Newport News, John Edwards of the Smithfield Times, Mrs. Richard F. Gundry of Hampton, Dr. Ronald E. Godby of Seaford, J. Lewis Rawls Jr. of Suffolk, Frank S. Brown of Norfolk Southern Corp., and Gilbert Francis of Southampton County, Phyllis Stephenson of Newport News; Helen Turner of Portsmouth and thorough copy editors Jill Vaden and Janet Molinaro.

Louis D. Rubin Jr. of Algonquin Books and Ruth Walker, book review editor, advised on every phase of the publication. Lloyd Davies of W.M. Brown and Son and Gus Dietz of Dietz Press went beyond duty, and a gifted designer and good companion, Alan Jacobson, made the most of the splendid photographs.